SELECTED ESSAYS MOSTLY ON BUDDHISM AND GANDHISM

SELECTED ESSAYS MOSTLY ON BUDDHISM AND GANDHISM

RAVINDRA KUMAR

Gyan Publishing House
New Delhi-110002

Selected Essays Mostly on Buddhist and Gandhism

ISBN : 81-212-0932-3
Rs. 340

Published in 2007 in India by
Gyan Publishing House,
5, Ansari Road, Daryaganj, New Delhi-110002
Phones : 23282060, 23261060
Fax : (011) 23285914
E-mail : books@gyanbooks.com
Website : www.gyanbooks.com

Laser Type-setting by : Shagun Graphics, Delhi
Printed at : Salasar Imaging System, Delhi

CONTENTS

SELF-UTTERANCE

Along with the invitation by the University of Sarajevo, Bosnia Herzegovina, to deliver some special lectures on Buddhism, Gandhism, Hinduism and other subjects related to peace, I was requested to prepare a manuscript from texts of all of them under a suitable title, so that the University could take initiative of its translation and publication into Bosnian language.

To accede to the request of the University, I gave a thought and finally prepared the manuscript under the title, ***SELECTED ESSAYS: MOSTLY ON BUDDHISM AND GANDHISM*** and before handing it over to the University for translation and publication into Bosnian, I also decided its publication into English language.

In this manuscript, more than a dozen texts are included. Although most of the texts are based on welfaristic philosophies of Buddhism and Gandhism, but the rest, especially on Morality, Non-Violence and Sufism, are also important and worth giving a thought.

I am thankful to those all who have extended their co-operation and help in preparation of this manuscript, especially Mr. Sachin Bathla, Ms. Kamlesh Kumar, Mr. S. P. Garg, Dr. Mridul Garg, Mr. Naresh Saini and Prof. Ranjana Yadunandan Chawada in reading the proofs; Mr. B. P. Garg, for undertaking the publication of it courageously; and Ms. Leena Bansod, for her continuous support and encouragement.

I do hope that after publication, readers in general and peace-lovers in particular, will find it useful and interesting.

—Ravindra Kumar

Bungalow 23-B, Lane: 2,
Mansarovar, Civil Lines,
MEERUT-250001 [India]
E-mails: ***ravindrakumar5@rediffmail.com***
ravindrakumar5@hotmail.com
ravindrakumar5@sify.com

1

BUDDHISM AND HINDUISM IN THE TWENTY-FIRST CENTURAY

Along with continuous development, pleasure, prosperity and peace constitute the essence of human life. Our progress, to any extent, in scientific and technical fields must be considered futile if it does not lead us to a life of pleasure, prosperity and peace. Of course, this very progress can be considered wholly meaningful in case it accords a development, intermingled with pleasure and prosperity, which ultimately leads on to the pathway of peace.

It has been more than a hundred years that technology began to emerge after science. The process of development in technology advanced rapidly. It is needless to mention its present status. The order is perpetually continuing. The Twentieth Century has already gone by and we have entered in the Twenty-First Century. Certainly, we find ourselves full of a new enthusiasm. But we should keep on going after grasping that essence of life, which we have well forgotten. Knowingly or non-knowingly, we are indifferent towards those *Sanatana* values, which ensure continuous development with pleasure, prosperity and peace. These values are eternal. They constitute the essence of life. Human religion is based on them. Hindu and Buddhist philosophies continuously reiterated these values before Human society. These values were predominant in sermons of those who basically preached *Vedic*-Hinduism. These very values were also the essence of sermons of Lord Buddha.

We should keep on going in the Twenty-First Century with a constant desire towards progress, prosperity and pleasure as peace and progress are the ultimate goals of human life. We should also realize the hope and with that our progress, prosperity and pleasure must be in right direction. Sphere of these should not be limited or short as we have to achieve peace as per a cherished way in this regard. The leading Propounders of Hinduism and Buddhism showed that way. They practically worked on the values that were capable to make this way constantly easy.

If we look at in the context of the Twenty-First Century, Hindu and Buddhist ideologies and religious-communities can very significantly contribute towards peace and progress incase they adopt fundamental values. In other words, both shall have very significant contribution in the process of peace and progress. Both of them are fully poised at playing an important role. They can accord a direction, which is termed as '*all-welfaristic.*' Although, the other religious- communities also, more or less, recognize these fundamental values, but Hindu and Buddhist ideologies consider them to be the foremost. And not only the foremost, every one of them was and is considered by them a religion in itself. We can say on this very accord that Hindu and Buddhist Communities and Philosophies shall be playing a very significant role along with these fundamental values towards peace and progress. These values are eternal. As such, they will guide humanity towards a true and real pathway, not only in relation to the Twenty-First Century, but also the future of both these ideologies and religious-communities shall remain bright while imbibed with these values.

Only a man can enjoy the fruits of progress, but when? Only when his existence is safe guarded. Not only this, but even in safe guarded existence his life should cross the walls of progress invariably with peace. Science and technology have made human life easy in various ways. But the events of Hiroshima and Nagasaki or the episode relating to Vietnam after the Second World War, were absolutely in human. To emphasize, wherever the development and advancement of science and technology was utilized like this, it was definitely against the humanity. In case if it is utilized in the same manner today, it cannot be justified on any ground, what so ever. The Supremacy of human values must remain intact.

Hindu and Buddhist ideologies and religious-communities, for this very reason, show a unique and exemplary path of human existence that is based on equality, along with a call for progress and peace. This path passes through compassion, non-violence and sacrifice. Let us tread this path. Along with that, let us discuss Hindu and Buddhist ideologies in context of compassion, non-violence and sacrifice, especially when we have entered in the Twenty-First Century.

KARUNA-THE COMPASSION

Karuna-the compassion is the first of the fundamentals of human religion established by Gautama Buddha. Compassion is that feeling, which incorporates *Maitri*-the friendliness in it. It is contradictory to depicting *Daya*-the pity, on someone along with a feeling of superiority over him. For example, let us consider a hungry and thirsty person who is taken to be so-called inferior in any respect. That so-called inferior person devotes himself to someone who is considered to be higher as he comes from a [so-called] higher class. Subsequently, he requests the so-called high to have pity on him so as to save him from hunger and thirst. Now, observing him, the so-called high person put two loaves of bread in the hands of the so-called low or quenches his thirst with some water from a utensil and the so-called low proceeds towards his destination after feeling well and satisfied. This is an act of mercy [pity] on the part of the so-called high as shown towards the so-called low. This feeling clearly attributes by the person showing pity while considering himself to be superior. It does not reveal *Karuna*-the compassion because compassion is antagonistic to it.

If, in case the so-called high person could be good enough to have the low seated with him, could give him bread in some utensil or could give a pot of water unto him, this all was to be an indication of his friendly feeling. Along with this, if the so-called high one could say some sweet words while giving meals and water, the friendly spirit could be more forceful, and this very spirit was full of compassion.

Compassion incorporates equality and humanity. Both the *Vedic*-Hindu and *Boddh* communities consider compassion to be a religion in itself. The leading person of these communities practiced compassion in their lives. Going of *Maryada-Purushottama* Lord Rama to abode of *Bhillini*-Shabari, taking her blessings and eating plums already tasted by her is an exquisite example of compassion. Not only is this, washing of Sudama's feet by Lord Krishna is another excellent example of compassion.

Tathagata Gautama Buddha also put several examples of compassion before us. His brother Devdutta had wounded a swan by an arrow. But the Buddha, as we all know, saved that swan, and through this, his feeling of compassion imbibed with protection can be well understood. In case Gautama Buddha was good enough only to the extent of setting the swan at liberty after proper dressing, subsequent to its release from Devdutta, it was an act of his mercy on the bird. But the Buddha did not do that. He lifted the wounded swan. He saved it from clutches of Devdutta. He constantly applied medico-solution to its affected part. He made it fully healthy and nourished it fraternally. In this act, it was his compassion full of equality and non-violence apart from fraternity.

As such, compassion is more stable than pity. The pity is fully transitory as we have noted through the conduct of high persons towards the so-called low who provided him meals, quenched his thirst and...? The low took his way. Compassion is permanent. Lord Rama sat near to *Bhillini*-Shabari. He ate plums already tasted by her. He stayed at her cottage. Their hearts touched each other. It was an inner togetherness and there could be a high record of equality.

The pity can be transformed into compassion, but when? Only when, a human being grasps equality in toto. Equality shall create the feeling of friendliness. In addition to it, the spirit of self-conceit shall perish. In compassion shown by Prince Siddhartha, there is no place to inequality, self-conceit and superiority complex. At any rate, inequality stands in contrast to humanity. In case pity is accorded while not giving up the feeling of inequality, it will also be indicative of enmity towards humanity. In case pity is tendered while keeping the spirit of equality at heart, it will clearly specify friendship. Such a pity shall be *Karuna*-the compassion. Such kind of pity shall be a true one; it will be full of humanity.

Gautama Buddha relieved compassion of hatred completely, propounding it as the essence of human religion. In case someone possesses the feeling of pity, it can be transformed in the *Karuna* of the Buddha when the person possessing that feeling makes it void of hatred. Contradictorily, if a person with hatred or abhorrence happens to express pity at any time, it can never take place of compassion. The pity can be compassion only when it is devoid of abhorrence. Gautama Buddha conveyed this very message. This message was conveyed by forerunners of the Hindu Religious-Community. In this regards a person can be compassionate only if he completely becomes free from the feeling of unfriendliness, inequality, abhorrence and violence.

As stated, compassion is not only in fully consonance to non-violence, in fact, the mother of compassion is non-violence itself. In Buddhism, compassion occupies a higher place than to non-violence in practice. The touching virtues of the both-non-violence and compassion-can are clearly understood in context of human-suffering. Non--violence is a natural virtue that obstructs the creation of sufferings. In contrast, compassion uproots the pain caused by suffering. In a situation when non-violence may be unsuccessful in obstructing the creation of suffering, compassion shall invariably alleviate the pain caused by violence. Peruse an example in this regard. An animal is poised to pull a cart that is fully loaded. The animal is not capable enough to pull it. The person in-charge on the cart intends to get it pulled by that very animal in any case. He makes the animal subject to vivid sufferings and tortures on this account. The animal is not at all capable to pull the cart in spite of so much suffering. Ultimately, it sits down; takes the ground. The cart man leaves the place after abandoning the animal in that condition of thirst and hunger and considering it as good for nothing. Another person comes that way. He finds the animal in pitiable condition. A sentiment rises in him. First of all, he takes the animal at a place devoid of sunlight, he gives it water; he feeds it. He goes to the extent of keeping it with him. The first person, who was aspiring to get the cart pulled by the animal through violent means, left it in a state where only pity could work. The second person was compassionate; he took it with him in a friendly spirit endowed with pity. The second one's pity imbibed with friendliness was, thus, compassion. In this situation, non-violence was also there with compassion as a supportive. Contrary to it, the pity depicted by the first one after violence was momentous. Violence has no place in a state of compassion also. In case the first one was compassionate, he could certainly refrain himself from loading unto the animal beyond its capability. Subsequently, he could not allow himself to force the animal to pull the cart by using violent means. In that case he could not leave it hungry and thirsty owing to it being unable to pull the cart.

Therefore, Gautama Buddha emphasized on compassion in terms of common welfare. His emphasis was in practical manner also. He associated non--violence with it. He himself was called a highly compassionate. I would like to make it clear that compassion can never originate in a state of fearfulness. After realization of agony or pain, real concern towards its eradication is compassion. This acts as a bridge in establishing permanent friéndship in humanity. As we have just now perused the example of Prince Siddhartha in context of a swan, at what point we come to, out of that? We get the point that he was compassionate right from his early stage of life. He said to Devdutta, "*Brother! Will you kill only innocent animals-deer-rabbit etcetera for hunting?*" He took in his lap the swan, injured by Devdutta's arrow, out of this spirit of compassion. He subsequently dispiayed friendliness towards it. He gave it water to have it out of pain. In his young age, he had seen an old man. He was unable to walk. Afterwards, he happened to see the dead body of a person. Some people were carrying the body to perform last rites. It is said that there was a transformation in his heart after seeing this. He was never fearful in a state of heart-transformation. He was only worried on account of birth, old age, hunger and death. Additionally, he was worried on account of general agony. He could not find ways to eradicate these concerns in case he was fearful.

In his times, *Kolis* and *Shakyas*-the two communities of *Khasttriyas*, were at daggers drawn owing to the dispute pertaining to distribution of water of Rohini River. There was a state of serious struggle between them for this reason. *Shakyamuni* was never fearful on account of this. He was, of course, concerned. He was aware that many people from both the sides would be killed when at war; this would inflict discomfort on soldiers and their family-members; there would be economic disaster; human society would be under the evil effects of war. And that's why; he made all out efforts to avert the war owing to this state of compassionate concerns. It was all because he embodied compassion wholly towards erasing human-agony. Even today a lot can be learnt from it by those who are concerned of people's problems and agonies, and especially by those who wish of peace along with progress.

It is known to all that spirit of compassion strengthened in Princes Siddhartha along with *Buddhatva*; he was a fully compassionate as soon as he became Buddha, that is, a person with enlightenment. Out of ten *Paramitas*, he put it at ninth as *Karunaparamita*. During his entitlement-period he put a stress on compassion more than any other *Paramita*. He also put it in his behaviours sumptuously. After enlightenment he was first of all fully compassionate towards those five *Jatilas* who deserted him saying that he was disgraced on account of eating *Kheer* offered by Sujata.[1] After attaining knowledge, the Buddha, first of all, taught those very five the lesson of the *Dhamma*. Giving up abhorrence, the five put themselves at his feet out of compassion. An example of his compassion is clear in his Dhamma teachings to Suneet. Also it can be grasped from his message for a life dedicated to the welfare, service and happiness of all. In the same manner, the compassion shown by Lord Rama towards Shabari, who was born in a so-called low heritage, is identical to this example. It was symbolical of Lord Rama's complete compassion. Lord Rama did not grasp the distinction of caste, creed or sex. He considered Shabari as an equal human-being. He identified her like his mother, showered his compassion, conveyed the knowledge of *Navadhabhakti* in simple manner and thus relieved her of agony.

Lord Rama's compassion towards Jatayu is an excellent example too. He not only embraced Jatayu, but also took away its agony. There are several other examples in which we can peruse Lord Rama's compassion clearly.

Suneet was born in a sweeper-family. Condition of Indian Society was poor in Lord Buddha's era. Caste system was there in its ghastly form. The so-called high class persons used to live separately. The villages were named in the names of *Brahmins* and *Chandalas*. The *Chandalas* were considered untouchable and unworthy of seeing. One day Lord Buddha was on his way. Seeing him, Suneet [sweeper] who was engaged in his work, gave him way after standing in a position that was at his cart's cover. He did so as he wished that Lord Buddha should not become impure by his sight. Lord Buddha, however, could see Suneet. He asked Suneet to be near to him. Afterwards, he took him to his *Sangha*, and thus honoured him. This was his feeling of friendliness along with that of pity. Even today this example is worth giving a thought especially by those who desire to make human-society united and strong and also by those who are worried of division of Indian Society into thousands of Castes and Sub-castes.

There is an example of Patachara also. She had lost her mental balance owing to death of her children, husband and parents. She was seen roaming nakedly in a state of lunacy. She could be seen shouting and abusing also. One day she reached the place where Gautama Buddha was preaching. Seeing her audiences was at alarm. The Buddha was a great psychologist; he grasped the mental-state of Patachara. He put his *Cheevar* on Patachara and said, "***Sister! Be conscious.***" Patachara was very much gay to hear such friendly and compassionate words. She stooped at Buddha's feet. The *Shakyamuni* admitted her as his disciple; he imparted education of the *Saddharma* to her. In the same way, he educated Aamrapali-the *Nagarvadhu* of Vaishali, with friendliness and also to Angulimal, who was indulged in inhuman activities for years. His compassion was very affective. And that is why; the rich distributed their wealth amongst the poor, exploited and down-trodden. *Shreshthiputras* like Anathapindika gave up attachment and greed. He donated all his property to *Bhikshuka-Sanghas*. Bonded labourers were freed by their masters. Mothers accorded permission gladly to their sons to join *Bhikshuka-Sanghas* of *Tathagata* Gautama Buddha. The women set their husbands at liberty to join the Sangha. Everywhere there was a talk about Buddha:

"Karunaaseetala Hridayam Panjaapajota Vihata Muhattamam;

Sanaraamara-Lokagurum Vande Sugato Gati Vimuttam." [1]

Meaning thereby: One whose heart is cool; in whose inner self the light of eternal -knowledge is emerged and there is elimination of darkness, originated by attachment, and he who is a universal teacher and is free from worldly disasters, I bowing salute that *SUGATA TATHAGATA BUDDHA*.

Shakyamuni Gautama, the ocean of compassion, spent approximately forty-five years of his life towards spreading immortal message of compassion to the people in general. He said to his *Bhikshukā* disciples:

"Charatha Bhikkhane Chaarakan Bahujana Hitaaya,

Bahujana Sukhaaya, Loka Anukampaaya,

Atyaaya Hitaaya, Sukhaam Deva Manussanam."[2]

To say:

"Oh Bhikshukas! Wander but only for the welfare of people, to make the people happy and prosperous."

Impressed by the compassion of the Buddha many of his disciples gave up all that they had. They dedicated themselves to the activities relating to human- welfare. They went to the places which were not easily accessible and propagated the message of *Karuna-Dhamma*. They crossed every barrier including mountains and seas. Their aim and objective remained to rid people of agonies through compassion.

There is no alternative to the activities prescribed by Lord Buddha and the leading propounders of the *Vedic*-Hindu-Community like Lord Rama, Lord Krishna etc. A Hindu saint has described pity to be the root of religion, but... ! The pity should be well-connected with friendliness and inequality. Merely pity-feeling is not wholly adequate. The establishment of the real pity is possible only with the spirit of equality. The foremost and significant message of Hinduism and Buddhism is the compassion at all levels-individual, social, national and international. This message was conveyed to us by our great propounders--Lord Rama, Lord Buddha etc.-who gained it by their toughest possible endeavours.

In the establishment of equality, Hindu and Buddhist communities and ideologies symbolize pity imbibed with friendliness. Both are immortal on this very account. Both have a very bright future perpetually.

SACRIFICE

Another fundamental of *Vedic*-Hinduism and Buddhism is the sacrifice. Sacrifice is that characteristic which continuously broadens heart of a person. Not only this, sacrifice indeed pursues a person towards path of duty. A real worthy life is not possible without sacrifice.

Yogishwara Krishna told Arjuna the secret of sacrifice in his immortal message of the *Gita*. In my view sacrifice is the essence of immortal message that was accorded to doubtful Arjuna by Lord Krishna. I mean to say that sacrifice is really a truth. We can perform a duty only through sacrifice. As such we should struggle for up-keeping humanity by giving up attachment towards family, clan or relatives etc. Arjuna grasped this and sacrificed family, teacher, clan, relatives and every other thing for up-keeping the human society. He struggled for truth.

Sacrifice of Prince Siddhartha was unique. Let us peruse that night when Prince Siddhartha went to sleeping-apartment of his wife-Yashodhara. There he saw that the room was bright with earthen-lamps that were full of scent. Yashodhara was sleeping sweetly and there were flowers all around her. One of her hands was on tender face of a small child. That scene was that of comfort and pleasure of high order. Siddhartha was inclined to lift his child affectionately for a time. He was going to sacrifice worldly pleasures. He suddenly stopped. He thought, ***"The mother of the child can awake."*** He was afraid that after awakening, she may pray to him and his heart may not remain firm enough. He was afraid that his determination might be obstructed. Considering so, he went out of the palace silently with a cool temper. In a moment that superman sacrificed his rights, high limitations, pleasant spirit of affection, and beautiful wife with a child, sleeping covered by her breasts. He treaded the path of sacrifice of very high order and was all out to this end as a poor traveler, who had deserted his household. This was an excellent example of self-oriented sacrifice. Thereafter, he made his sacrifice constant. At a time, he again had a desire to be with his wife and his six year old son. He was also cherishing to return to the kingdom and to be with his parents. But, he was not satisfied with this all. He thought, ***"What would happen to the vow in which I have dedicated myself with a sense of sacrifice?"*** This very thought made him firm. Sacrifice was incorporated in his firmness. He was determined to achieve his goal. Prince Siddhartha initiated the above-mentioned spirit of self-sacrifice with curiosity. There was darkness in the way, but he inculcated complete firmness. Ultimately, all doubts were eliminated. The light of truth emerged owing to and out of sacrifice. This was beyond comprehension of academics. Such a truth could not be realized at academic considerations. This was also not possible through meditation or penance alone. It was only sacrifice that could put truth clearly to be comprehended. Prince Siddhartha became the Buddha; the Buddha learnt the art of a sacred life through sacrifice. He also got the knowledge of compassion, affection and human-equality. After sacrifice, big hearted Buddha had known that affection towards every living being is the best way to self-attainment. He prescribed sacrifice to be indispensable ingredient of human religion. Subsequently, he constantly increased dedication to sacrifice unto his inner self. He declared:

"One who has finished his [worldly] travel, who has given up feeling of grief completely, has liberated himself by relieving of all chains in every way, only he can overcome of sorrows; he only can be free from all kinds of bounds."[3]

After the enlightenment, the compassionate Gautama searched out the way to put an end to the human suffering, and in this regard he accorded a message, ***"If a person reaches this stage of sacrifice in life, he achieves real aim of life. This is the stage of highest pleasure in human life. Desire of things is the root cause of all evils. In contrast, human salvation is based on sacrifice. We shall have to give up thirst, i.e. undue desire. We shall have to march towards freeing ourselves."***

In the words of the Buddha:

"Tam Vo Vadaami Bhadda Vo, Yaavantettha Samaagataa;

Tanhaaya Moolam Punappuna, Usarittho Va Veeranam;

Maa Vo Nala, Va Soto Vam Maro Bhanji Punappunam" [4]

It means:

"On this account, I speak to all of you, who are here, about your welfare. As we uproot the grass for Khus, in the same manner you take out the root of desire; you should give up thirst fully. In case you do not do that you will be regularly doomed by the Mara."

As known to all, thirst, i.e., desire is the root cause of agony, according to Gautama Buddha. Desire, i.e., *Trishna* has three forms-*Kama*, *Bhava* and *Vibhava*. This is originated by the contact of six senses-*Chakshu*, *Shrota*, *Ghrana*, *Jivha*, *Kaya* and *Mana* and their six subjects–*Roopa*, *Shabda*, *Gandha*, *Rasa*, *Sparsha* and *Vigyana* [also called *Samskara*]. To say, eyes and skin realize charm and beauty. Ears hear sweet words. Nose realizes intoxicating smell. The body stimulates. Resultantly, thirst pertaining to lust originates. In order to get achieved and realized *Trishna*, and its very desire, will give place to oneness or separation, desperation and sadness as per an unfamiliar way. Thirst is to be given up invariably as such. Giving an example Lord Buddha said:

"Conception takes place when three meet. Firstly, mother and father are at togetherness. Secondly, mother is at cycle. Thirdly, Gandharva marks its presence. After conception, mother gives birth to child after a gap of nine to ten months. Then

she brings the child up by milk from her body. The child begins to proceed towards youth. He plays with toys like Bunka, Mouth-lattoo, Chingulia, Tula, Cart, Dhanuhi etc. After attaining age, he enjoys senses--Roopa, Rasa, Shabda, Gandha and Sparsha. He realizes pleasure or pain according to pro or anti stage of the above. In a state of pleasure he bends to greet things. This greeting produces Nandi-[Trishna] in him. This Trishna itself is the desire to gain things as in context of various sufferings."

Trishna is very dreadful. It is only for lust that a King takes up confrontation with Kings, a brave with braves, a *Brahmin* with *Brahmins* and a *Grihapati* [*Vaishya*] with *Grihapatis* [*Vaishyas*]. Mother quarrels with her son and sons quarrel with mother. Father is at confrontation with his own son and sons are at daggers drawn against their own father. A brother fights with sister and vice versa. Brothers and friends quarrel together and attack each other with arms in a stage of arguments and perplexity. This causes even death unto them and gives place to agonies that are equivalent to that.

Substantially, *Trishna*, which is caused by our mal-desires happens to be the cause of our agonies and deserves to be abandoned. It should be given up, as much as possible, on personal, social, national or international planes and also at the level of family through the Middle-

Way. A person entangled in *Trishna* can give it up by his conduct to the maximum possible extent only through the Middle-Way. Gautama Buddha called upon the people to give up *Trishna* through eightfold Middle-Way-*Samyak-Drishti*, *Samkalpa*, *Vanee*, *Karma*, *Aajivikaa*, *Vyaayaama*, *Smriti* and *Samaadhi*. It is a fact that the spirit of sacrifice is great. Values like those of non-violence and compassion strengthen in proportion to a man's up-gradation as per his coming out of the worldly spheres. Love, friendliness and equality gradually develop when these values are there. Regular enhancement of these indicates humanity and they must essentially and continuously be realized. Gautama Buddha said:

"Krodham Jahe Vippa Jaheyya Maana Sanaujanam Sabbamatikkameyya;

Tam Naama Rupasmi Asanjamaanam Akinchanam Naanupatanti Dukkha" [5]

It means:

"A person who is non-attached by giving up desires and who has broken all chains by sacrificing anger and pride, he never suffers."

The sacrifice is fully capable of saving this world from doom. That is why; Gautama Buddha considered sacrifice to be very significant. He considered it to be most helpful up to the door of the *Moksha*. Vadnarayana Vyasa had told to Aamrapali in this regard:

"When you peruse that all is not well with the Republic, take up some great sacrifice and all shall be well."

As described earlier, *Tathagata* Gautama himself presented many examples based on sacrifice for an exquisite and successful life. Those examples were in the form of messages; they were very simple and straightforward. No one can deny their reality, truthfulness or consonance. Through them, a person shall certainly proceed towards the pathway of the *Dhamma*. Buddha did not consider worldly deeds or indulgence in them sufficient for self-progress. But, to what extent? Till then the deeds often do not incorporate spirit of sacrifice; and that is too especially true for house-holders. As such, daily practices must be carried out keeping of the following five kinds of sacrifice in mind:

A-SEPARATION OF SPIRIT OF VIOLENCE

It means that a creature should not be killed; it should also not be got killed. One who kills some other should not be appreciated. Killing must be opposed and contradicted in respect of every creature, small or big, mighty or weak. Any attempt towards killing should also be opposed.

B-SEPARATION OF THINGS NOT BELONGING TO SELF

It means that *Shravaka*, i.e., a Monk should not take anything, which has not been given to him. In case someone is trying to take anything as such, he should be prohibited. If one succeeds to gain a thing in such a manner, he should be denied approval for that. Everything gained by theft is a subject of being given up.

C-SEPARATION OF ADULTERY

A human being should give up adultery that is resultant of lust and is like a burning coal. His prudence can be perused in such an act. Even if he cannot control his senses he should not enter into relations with a woman who is not his wife.

D-SEPARATION OF FALSEHOOD

A person should separate him from every kind of falsehood. He should not speak anything, which is not true. He should also not instigate any other to tell a lie. A person, telling a lie, should not be appreciated. It is also incumbent on a person to refrain himself from speaking very much in an assembly or at court. It is never graceful to speak excessively.

E-SEPARATION OF INTOXICANTS

A householder must not consume intoxicants; he should not take any intoxicant himself and should also not serve it to any other. Anyone, who takes such a thing, should never win approval.

As such, the existence of a human being is safe only in a state of compassion imbibed with the spirit of sacrifice. It is on this account that the *Vedic*-Hindu and Buddhist Religious Communities accord emphasis on sacrifice. They not only accord emphasis in this regard, but also call upon others to do so. In the Hindu scriptures, an example of sacrifice by Laxmana is excellent one. He was not ordered to be in exile for fourteen years. He was never in the race of Kingship of Ayodhya, and even then he spent most important fourteen years of his young age in forests amidst struggles and turmoil. He had young and beautiful wife and exquisite things pertaining to majesty, but he was not knotted down by *Trishna* or attachment. He could do so only because he could comprehend that sacrifice is the supreme. *Maharishi* Valmiki gave up all attachments as soon as he attained knowledge of reality and truth. No *Trishna* could constrain him thereafter. He offered all his life for the welfare of humanity. Emperor Ashoka also gave up all attachments when he was at top of governance. He presented before the world an excellent example of living sacrifice. Hindu and Buddhist

Communities, thus, shall inspire the human-world on the basis of spirit of sacrifice.

AHIMSA

The third, but most significant basis of Hindu and Boddh Communities is *Ahimsa* the non-violence. Non-violence has been termed as *Parmodharma* in the *Vedic*-Hindu philosophy. The *Mahabharata* incorporates:

"Non-violence is the religion in grandeur, i.e. Parmodharma."[6]

The father of the *Vedic*-Hindu Law, Manu, considered *Ahimsa* to be a religion dedicated to the duty to be performed. According to Manu:

"Ahimsa Satyamasteyam,
Shauchamindriyanigrahah,
Etam Samasikam Dharma
Chaturvarenye Abraveeta Manuh."[7]

The *Yoga*, one of the prominent branches of *Vedic*-Hindu Philosophy also accords foremost position to *Ahimsa*. According to it:

"Ahimsa, Satya, Asteya, Brahmacharya, Aparigraha, Yamah,

Shaucha, Santosha, Tapah, Swadhyaya, Ishwara Pranidhanani Niyamah."[8]

It clarifies that the *Vedic*-Hindu Philosophy and Religious-Community considered *Ahimsa* to be foremost and significant. It is because the existence of humanity fully depends upon *Ahimsa*. There is a description in human-history that our ancestors had been eating each other. Afterwards they adopted hunt of animals. They began to be abhorred at killing each other from amongst themselves. Thereafter, they began to feel ashamed at being alive on the basis of hunting. They began to dig soil and resultantly they got different kind of food; and now it was prosperity in jungles. They cherished to be at a place in a spirit of togetherness and did not like to wander hither and thither. The villages and cities emerged. Spirit of family life took place in human beings and this very spirit in them transformed itself into formation of the society. This clarifies that *Ahimsa* has been very significant for human existence and development. In case it was otherwise, like many other creatures of low profile, human beings could have also reached to end. It was for this reason that Gautama Buddha also considered *Ahimsa* to be significant for human existence and progress. He prescribed:

"Sukhakaamaani, Bhootaaniyoon, Danden, Vinhinsati,

Attanon Sukha Mesano Pechcha So Na Labhate Sukham;

Sukhakamaani Bhootani Ya Dandena Na Himsati,

Attano Sukhamesaano Pechcha Sa Labhate Sukham" [9]

It Means:

"One who aspires for happiness, and for this induces sufferings on others, even after his death, he cannot be at comfort. Contrary to it, one who does not kill others for his pleasure remains at happiness and peace even after the death."

Ahimsa is not confined to causing or inflicting pain on any living being or reducing to death. In it, violence of mind, tongue and action, all three, are prohibited. This spirit inspires a man towards sacrifice. It provides a message of friendliness. Not only this, presence of *Ahimsa* and thereby constant sacrifice or abandonment of violence is essential for human existence. *Ahimsa* can be perfect only when it is '*Manasa*, *Vacha*, and *Karmana*'. Gautama Buddha propagated non-violence for humanity in the same manner, i.e. as per mind, tongue and action, and for this purpose, keeping human-beings at the highest position, fixed a practical degree to the maximum possible extent. For example, *Tathagata* Gautama prohibited killing of human being; he also prohibited any attempt of causing mental or physical injury to any person. He prohibited exploitation or inflicting any pain on someone through harsh words; he opposed any such act, which may cause a shock on any person's mind or heart. He considered '*Manasa*, *Vacha*, *Karmana*' to be absolutely essential for *Ahimsa*. He accorded supreme position to a human being in the domain of *Ahimsa*. After that, man must be non-violent towards creatures as far as possible; and it is practicable. This is a call by Gautama Buddha. As already enunciated, he called on householders that a creature should not be killed and should not be caused to be killed. In case someone kills or attempts to kill a creature, he should not be applauded. A person should oppose killing of a creature-mighty or feeble. Naturally, life is dear to all. Gautama Buddha said:

"Sabbe Tasanti Dandasya Sabbe Bhaayaanti Machchuno,

Attaana Upama Katwa Na Haneyya Na Ghaataye;

Sabbe Tasanti Dandasma Sabbes Jeevitam Piyam,

Attaana Upama Katwaa Na Haneyya Na Ghaataye." [10]

It means:

"All creatures are fearful of punishment; all persons are fearful of death. Remember! You are alike them. As such, do not recourse to violence. Do not instigate others to involve in violence. All like life; and punishment is dreadful to all. As such, consider

everyone as equal and do not kill anyone. Do not even have a desire to kill [anyone]."

A person must practice non-violence up to the extent of its practical possibility. '***Paanaatipaataa Veramani, Sikkhapadamsamaadayaami***', the first ***Sheela*** states:

"I am to accede to the doctrine of refraining from violence towards any creature"

And this is the essence of Buddha's *Ahimsa*. There were two popular thoughts about violence and non-violence in his times. The first one was Braahamini. Based on conservative consideration, the Braahamini thought accepted sacrifice of human beings or animals at the *Yajnas*. Mainly cows, horses and bullocks etc. were killed for the purpose. The followers of the Braahamini believed in the theory that '***Vaidiki Himsa, Himsa Na Bhavati***', i.e. violence caused according to Vedic method cannot be termed violence. Lord Buddha did not agree to this thought. In this context he said:

"In case the creatures sacrificed at Yajnas are scheduled to be at heaven, those who say so must send to Heaven their family-members by sacrificing them as such at Yajnas."

This was a befitting answer to them. He continuously condemned such kind of conservative and inhuman considerations. Resultantly, such kind of sacrifices is almost negligible at the *Vedic*-Hindu Yajnas today.

Lord Buddha opposed killing of useful animals as per their being of use in agriculture and other fields of human society. He called upon humanity to protect animals. About cows, he said to *Brahmins* of Shravasti:

"They are our intimate friends. They should be considered like parents and we must have a fraternal attitude towards them. They provide us healing things."

Truly speaking, milk, butter and curd which we get from cows are like medicines. Her excreta is useful for fertilizing the soil and the same is useful as fuel. Her calves is boon to us as they work to plough the field. On such considerations, Lord Buddha sermoned *Ahimsa* and combined it with friendliness.

To follow *Ahimsa* to its last stage is extremely difficult. It seems impracticable that we should blame anyone for killing any creature: knowingly or unknowingly. Innumerable invisible and small flying creatures or those confined to earth-such as ants in a way and other small creatures are killed by people. A person is generally ignorant of such killings. As such, as far as possible, a person must not indulge himself into any violence deliberately. In other words, a person should practice

Ahimsa to the maximum possible extent of practicability. There is an example of Singh Senapati, which can be quoted in context of Buddha's practical *Ahimsa*. Senapati was a follower of *Vardhamana* Mahavira. He asked *Shakyamuni* Gautama:

"Even now, there is a doubt left within myself; may Lord accord a solution please? The doubt is that I am a Senapati of Armed forces. The King has appointed me to get statutes of state obeyed by the people and to participate in the war. In such a situation, will you permit to punish the evil-doers whereas you possess a spirit of pity and unlimited compassion towards those in distress? Will Tathagata also state that is it not proper to be at fight to save our homes, wives, offspring and property? Does your Lordship-Tathagata-accords a sermon of total surrender? Should a robber, who snatches forcefully, be allowed mental satisfaction and thereby be permitted to snatch all? Are all wars that are earmarked for justice, prohibited? What is the message of Tathagata in this regard and at such junctures?"

". . . Who is punishable, must be punished; one who deserves award, must be awarded".

Tathagata accorded a reply to Singh Senapati's all queries in one sentence. After that, *Tathagata* said:

"Now, Senapati has to decide that-it is incumbent on him to be certain as to what is to be offered to an evil-doer-punishment or award."

It is now clear that Gautama Buddha denied any feeling like that of violence in the form of attack for a selfish end. However, he never obstructed humanity to raise voice against injustice, sin, evil-doings etc. Truly speaking, these pursuits tend to oppose violent tendencies. On this account, the armed struggles undertaken by Lord Rama were meant to end violent tendencies. On this very consideration Lord Krishna had induced Pandavas to be at armed confrontation. These were the forms of practical non-violence. Lord Buddha stated regarding practical non-violence for this very reason. Man is competent to peruse practical non-violence himself. In case a lion or any other dreadful beastly animal attacks a person, he shall do everything in his defence, whatever he may be capable of doing. It is possible that the lion or some other beast may lose its life in this. This clears that safeguarding and hunting are two separate tendencies. One is non-violent as per tendency whereas the other is full of violent feeling. The essence is that human tendency should be non-violent. As far as possible, a person must practically exercise *Ahimsa*.

There is no place to non-fulfillment of one's duty under the cover of *Ahimsa*. Also *Ahimsa* is not related to cowardliness. The *Vedic*-Hindu and Boddh Communities oppose *Ahimsa* when it is based on non-dutiful spirit. Along with that, they oppose surrender before the one who creates any havoc. There is a good example of the time of Buddha himself. The King of Magadha, Bimbisaar, sent his General to counter the havoc in the frontier province. The General came to Buddha's *Sangha*. He was fearful and non-dutiful. He became a *Bhikshuka*. Bimbisaar merely complained about this to Lord Buddha. The Buddha clarified at that very moment:

"I never endorse such an act of any soldier who does so taking under the cover of non-violence and being devoid of dutifulness."

Not only this, he also declared:

"Oh Bhikshukas! Do not admit any state-soldier in the Sangha. In case any one does so, he will be guilty of misdeed."

Gautama Buddha did not admit any such person who came to his fold after overriding solemnity to safeguard his country, society or state. He did not accord membership to anyone who came to the *Sangha* after abandoning duty of war and holding position of a coward. It was Buddha's clear holding that every person should perform his oı her duty towards self, society and country.

It is clear that non-violence never comes in the way of a human being who carries out his duties.

Lord Buddha saved a swan from the clutches of Devdutta as he had a tendency of *Ahimsa*. Contrary to this, Devdutta hunted swan as he had a feeling of violence. Devdutta's feeling cherished violence without a reason and it collided with the *Ahimsa* that was within Prince Siddhartha. As such, human nature must be non--violent. Lord Krishna had also presented such an example and had said that even if only one non--violent way is available towards our goal, we should discard violence and adopt the non-violent one.

But, as we all know, a living being including a human being, can never be absolutely non-violent. For example, let us take violence pertaining to life or corporal factor. Let us put aside for a moment *Mana*, *Vachana* and *Karmas*. Violence takes place at meals, vivid activities and even at the process of breathing. As such, Hindu and Buddhist, both the philosophies accord emphasis on adoption of *Ahimsa* within a limit. Of course, one should not be a cause to violence. Even if there is necessity or no other way left out, a person must fully endeavour to abstain from becoming a cause to violence.

Shakyamuni Gautama was himself great example non-violence. There was non-violence in his conduct. He propagated *Ahimsa* in practical perspective in place of its impossible form. Lord Rama, Lord Krishna and other leaders of the Vedic- Hindu Religious Community also considered non--violence to be supreme and dictated to practice it as far as possible. Non-violence was there in their tendency and conduct. If human tendency is non--violent, he shall refrain himself from violence. This will constantly enhance the spirit of non-violence in him. Constant enhancement of spirit of non-violence shall ultimately pave a way to pleasure, prosperity and peace. As such, Hindu and Buddhist, both the Communities and ideologies, accord emphasis on totally practical non-violence. This is very useful and significant.

A farmer carries out functions related to agriculture. He ploughs the field for this purpose. He irrigates the crop. He indulges in hoeing work several times. While doing so, innumerable visible and invisible creatures are subjected to violence. There are so many insecticides. A farmer saves crop from insects after utilizing these things. He upbrings the world from that very crop; but a farmer never abstains from the duty to grow the crops as per a fear of creature-violence. The world shall die of hunger in case he does so. Not only this, milk of cow, buffalo, goat etc. is juice of their body. Innumerable invisible microbes float in it. But, human beings consume milk and utilize it in different forms. As such, non-violence must be acceptable to the maximum practical possibility. Today, botany stipulates that there is certainly violence at consumption of all the articles related to our meals.

A human being is superior to all other creatures. It is on this account that he stands supreme in the domain of non-violence. This is why that the *Vedic*-Hindu and *Boddh* Religious–Communities stress on adoption of practical aspect of non-violence to the maximum possible extent. This is indeed related to our welfare and well-being. Non-violence is a doctrine of life even after any such considerations. It is essential for peace and progress that non--violènt spirit must be spread in human life. A person practicing it casually or occasionally cannot be called a non-violent. This is the message of the *Vedic*-Hindu and *Boddh*–Communities.

Both, the *Vedic*-Hindu and Boddh Religious Communities call upon humanity to grasp immortal message of above-mentioned three prime values-compassion, sacrifice and non-violence. According to this call, these are greatly competent to contribute towards peace and progress. We should ponder over it in the Twenty-First Century whether there is any alternative to compassion, sacrifice and non-violence? And if the answer is 'No', we should make these three an essential part of our daily practices along with making progress in various spheres of Science or in the field of Technology and/or in other spheres. The existence of humanity and its golden future is most significant and as such, constant development of such spirits into it is essential.

Reference:

1. *According to a story in reference of Buddha, "He was dissatisfied with Ashrama of Acharya Aalar Kalam. Subsequently, he went to the Ashrama of Acharya Udraka, who was the head of seven hundred students of philosophy. Udraka wanted a bright and intellectual youth like Gautama to be in his Ashrama. Udraka urged Gautama to this effect. Gautama expressed desire for Abhisambodhi while with Acharya. Udraka accorded his philosophical knowledge to him in a phased manner but Gautama found it incomplete for Samyaka-Sambodhi. He departed himself from Acharya. When Gautama left, five students of Ashrama belonging to noble families also accompanied him. These five were very much impressed by non-comparable curiosity and bright intelligence of the Gautama. They considered Gautama to be a divine person and began to serve him devotedly. Gautama and all five of them reached at Gayasheersha mount after some days. While there, Gautama established that one should undergo penance in order to get wisdom. He reached Urubela in search of a suitable place for undergoing penance. At that time Urubela was near Niranjana River. Finding that place very graceful and fit for undertaking penance, Shakyamuni stayed there and began to undergo penance. The five students accompanying him began to talk about him when they observed him dedicated to penance. For six years Shakyamuni continuously underwent into penance there He caused vivid discomforts to his body. He remained hungry so as to reduce his white-complexioned body into a blackish one. Only skeleton was there now in his body. His eyes became static in sockets. The nose and ears dried up to the*

extent of being transparent. The body was reduced to a skeleton. Gautama focused his attention breathlessly as he was practicing three vital exercises, Rechaka, Kumbhaka and Pooraka. One day a situation was there when he was on the ground unconsciously owing to very painful feeling in the body. The five companions took the Gautama to have demised. However, it was not so. The Gautama was at stage of inexpressible eternity that was beyond considerations of life and death, and which surpassed all hitherto known situations in this regard. He came to the stage of Sangyat-Samadhi from that of above-mentioned critical stage of Agama-Mahasamadhi. He contemplated that Buddhatva shall not be gained out of severe penance. This is not the way to attain true knowledge in toto. He realized that a balanced life devoid of pains to body or bestowment of comforts unto it can only be adequate. After such contemplation, he symbolically expressed desire of some food and that desire was in this manner put by him before his companions. The companions cherished to give him water along with that also gave him lentil-juice. His body gained strength and subsequently he began to take alms in the villages. "It was during those days that Sujata, a daughter of Kakunavi-family of Sainani-village of Urubela-Province prayed to a Banyan-tree, "In case I am married to a bridegroom as handsome and worthy as myself and if I get a son out of my first pregnancy, I shall worship God-Banyan on ***Vaisakh-Poornima*** *every year. " Sujata had her desire fulfilled. She was bestowed with a handsome son. As per the promise, Sujata began to prepare herself to worship Banyan-tree. She awoke in the morning of Vaisakh-Poornima. She took milk out of her Kapila cows. Then, she began to prepare thick and nutritive sweet dish of rice and milk that is Kheer. Her maid Poorna was there when she was preparing the sweet dish. She sent Poorna to clean the ground under the Banyan tree. When Poorna reached to clean the ground under the Banyan* tree, she saw Gautama there at Samadhi to attain knowledge in toto. The Gautama was on Padmasana. Poorna also observed a divine light emerging out of white- complexioned body of the Gautama. Resultantly, the whole Banyan tree was shining. Poorna thought as if Banyan God was himself there in order to admit worships of her mistress. He is waiting for worship. She was very glad. She rushed to Sujata and told her everything. Hearing that God was waiting for worship, Sujata was overwhelmed with pleasure. Poorna was awarded.

"The rice and milk-made sweet dish, kheer, prepared with sacred love and sublime regard was served in a golden pot. It was covered with a beautiful new cloth. After that, she took a bath and wore new clothes. She put the pot on head and departed towards the tree with Poorna. She reached near the tree and saw there Gautama who was showering divine grace. She was gay. She also took the Gautama to be Banyan-God. The pot was taken down by her and thereafter she greeted him bending her head. Then, she opened the pot. She went up to him with a pot of water also; the pot was full of attractive scent out of scented flowers. She expressed a desire to accept her presentation. The Gautama comprehended the feeling that was there in Sujata. First of all, he presented his Bhikshapatra to accept her present, but thereafter, he did not give his pot but fully unfolded his both hands before her to get her pot of Kheer, and that of water. Sujata offered the pots to his hands. Then the Gautama saw at Sujata with his compassionate eyes. The five companions had been watching this episode. They apprehended as if Gautama was on the path of moral degradation as per enticement by a woman, however, fact was never this one. Resultantly, all the five left him. The Gautama engaged himself again towards finding out truth. When he attained knowledge, he pondered over... 'Who should be imparted this first of all? He also thought..."Who should be fortunate enough in respect of the knowledge gained? Aalar Kalam? No, perhaps he *might not be alive! Then Udraka! -He might also not be alive." After that he thought of those five who had left considering him immorally corrupt. Now Gautama Buddha decided to search them and to propagate the knowledge of the Dhamma in their vicinity. The Buddha reached Rishipattana Mrigdavo near Boddhagaya in their search. All five of them were residing there. Seeing Gautama coming towards them, they decided not to salute or respect him. They were of the view that Shramana Gautama was coming towards them after being corrupt; he had, now an aspiration for more gains, possessed a stout body of firm organs and appeared white-complexioned. Even though they considered him worthy of a seat as per belonging to upper class [of the society] and as such decided to offer him a seat. Their decision was trembling as soon as Gautama Buddha was approaching nearer. They formally saluted and offered regards to Buddha, but they could not respect him fully as they were ignorant of the knowledge in him. Subsequently, they were impressed by the knowledge of Gautama Buddha and consequently the Buddha could accord first sermon of the Dhamma to those five. It was an episode pertaining to compassion in him. It was owing to compassion that even though he was so far from them, he searched those doubtful and sad disciples and accorded knowledge to them. He taught them to indulge themselves towards welfare and happiness of human beings."*

2. *Shanti Ki Aur*, Volume 1, page 45
3. Same as above, page 45
4. Above, page 50
5. Above, page 52
6. *Mahabharata, Anushasana Parva.*
7. Non-violence and Its Philosophy, page 12
8. Same as above.
9. *Shanti Ki Aur*, Volume 1, page 55

10. Same as above, page 56

Bibliography:

- Cowell, E. B., *Mahayana* Buddhist Text, APD, New Delhi [India], 1990
- Dasgupta, Subbhayu, Hindu Ethics and the Challenge of Change, Arnold-Heinemann, Calcutta [India], 1977
- Gandhi, M. K., The Essence of Hinduism, Navajivan Publishing House, Ahmedabad [India], 1987
- Kumar, Ravindra, Gandhi and Gandhism, Part –I, World Peace Movement Trust, Meerut [India] 2001
- Kumar, Ravindra, Gaụtama Buddha and the *Dhammapada*, Kalpaz Publications, Delhi [India], 2007
- Kumar, Ravindra, Non-Violence and its Philosophy, Dynamic Publications, Meerut [India], 2003
- Kumar, Ravindra, Religion and World Peace, Gyan Publishing House, New Delhi [India], 2006
- Kumar, Ravindra, *Shanti Ki Aur*, Volume 1, Love & Co., Meerut [India], 2001
- Laxmanashastri, P. V., *Maharishi* Valmiki's *Yogavashishtha*, Part 1 & 2, Bombay [India], 1911-1937
- Manu, *Manusmriti*, Randhir, Hardwar [India], 1992
- Max Muller, F., The *Dhammapada*, Atlantic, New Delhi [India], 1990
- Tulsidas, Goswami, *Ramacharitamanasa*, Gita Press, Gorakhpur, 1963

****

2

PHILOSOPHY OF LIFE HIINAYAANA BUDDHISM IN PRACTICE TODAY

To make human life worthy, prosperous and peaceful, different philosophies and thoughts have been propounded through the ages, of which Buddhism occupies a prominent place. It is well evident from the fact that approximately five hundred million people all over the world carry out their day-to-day activities on the basis of Buddhist doctrines. The Buddhist Religious-Community has fourth place amongst the major religious-communities of the world. [1]

In quite simple and clear words, Buddhism consists of that great and all-welfaristic philosophy of life, which, especially Gautama Buddha put forth before human world[2] approximately two thousand five hundred years ago, and having *Karuna*-the compassion, a value supplementary to *Ahimsa*-the non-violence in the centre, treated his individual life in accordance with it.

Karuna-the compassion is not merely a word close to pity as it is generally understood. Like *Ahimsa*, it, too, involves a wider concept. It is, in fact, an abridgement of pity and friendliness; in it, there is an urge for perpetual need of equality based on affection and friendliness.

Gautama Buddha was fully aware of that consideration in which a person desired to control others; he wanted to keep him in higher position in comparison to others. The Buddha, a great *Guru*- the teacher with great mind was also aware that this factor had been responsible for disintegration of society and the nation. And that's why he, having *Karuna* nucleus, emphasized on equality amongst all human beings-men and women, and there was no caste or class in his vocabulary.

Till the last breath, Gautama Buddha tried to make human beings understand that surety of existence could be possible if the path of equality was followed; progress could be made if the desire of becoming master was given up; peace could be achieved if human beings, knowing the reality, control themselves and they become compassionate by heart and soul.

II

Hiinayaana is one of the prominent schools of thoughts of Buddhism. Generally, it is believed that the *Hiinayaana* thoughts are individualistic. Maximum stress of *Hiinayaana* is to take a human being towards happiness and salvation or liberation, or *Nirvana* from his personal sufferings or grieves, or *Dukhas*, by creating full understanding and reality of the Four Noble Truths or the *Arya- Satya* in him, and through the unique Eightfold Path.

Many amongst scholars of both-the East and the West-have also extended an argument that because *Hiinayaana* philosophy is centralized upon individual, it is micro in dimension; and it is for this reason perhaps that it has been linked to word '*hiina*', which in simple words can be translated to '*lesser*', '*small*' or '*low*'.

But in reality, despite being centralized on individualism, the message and objective of *Hiinayaana* philosophy is neither small nor its depth can be underestimated; especially because not only in the East, rather Western scholar like Gene Hopp also agrees:

"Hiinayaana Buddhism is a good introduction [itself] of Buddhism what the Buddha [himself] taught".

Many verses of the *Dhammapada* clarify the above realty, and the following *Pada* of them demands special attention in this context:

"Do not forget [to] him for the sake of others', however great [they are]; care for self first and then adhere to the welfare of all."[13]

Along with this, other verses, which may be quoted in support of the argument, are from the *Puppha Vaggo*, the *Sahassa Vaggo* and the *Brahamana Vaggo*.

In the 50eth verse [*Puppha Vaggo*][4], Gautama Buddha says:

"A man must look at his own misdeeds or negligence, and not of others' sins or faults; he must not take notice of others' [ill] words."

Similarly, *Tathagata* [through verses 104 and 105] of the *Sahassa Vaggo*][5] has conveyed the message:

"One's own [self] conquered is better than to conquer others. One who conquers himself, and it restrained, he, indeed, is a good [man]" and ***"One who conquers himself, he cannot be defeated [even] by a god, by a Gandharva, or by Mara, or by Brahman."***

Simultaneously, *Shakyamuni* Gautama emphasized upon self purification by self-beginning [through verses 158-159 of the *Dhammapada*][6] says:

"Let [a man] indulge himself first to what is good [act] and then let him teach [the same] to others; doing this, a wise and intelligent will not suffer. Let him make proper first to what he wants to teach others; control himself first before directing others [to do so]. In fact, one's own self subdue is difficult."

And lastly, his preaching that 'man is himself his master; no other one can be his master; and rare mastership is gained only after sublimating oneself adequately', can also is seen in this very context.[7]

Now, after analyzing above verses, what conclusion appears before us? Is the *Hiinayaana* philosophy really an individualistic one or is it micro in dimension, or is it centralized upon individualism? Not, as I think and believe.

Reality is this that *Hiinayaana* philosophy was in existence even before the *Mahaayaana*, another prominent branch of Buddhism; may be not in the name of *Hiinayaana*, because nomenclature Hiinayaana came to light at the time of rising of *Mahaayaana* during a broad philosophical discourse on Buddhist philosophy, which took place after Lord Buddha. Nevertheless, *Hiinayaana* was discovered as a rival word by a great intellectual belonging to the *Mahaayaana* school of thought. May be or may not be that great intellectual might have meant to downgrade its rival philosophy in comparison to their own views and for this reason he called it *Hiinayaana* [lesser vehicle]. Even then, *Hiinayaana* is not a lesser vehicle; as it is important and relevant even today.

As is well known, Lord Buddha also accepted the principle of enjoying or suffering the consequences of one's actions. He agreed that humans are liable to the destiny according to one's deeds. Buddha declared the human deeds as the reason of repeated birth-death and rebirth and accepted deed itself as the basis of ultimate salvation. The principle of four noble truths [*Dukha*-

suffering, source of *Dukha*, cessation of *Dukha* and the path of cessation of *Dukha*] expounded by him, firstly shows the fact [mirror] of human life and then provides point wise knowledge and intelligence to make it purposeful and fruitful. Not only has this, Lord Buddha's call for determined adaptation and specific commitments and promises for development of ideal virtues, especially *Shila*-the moral conduct [which is literally linked to calmness and pleasantness], also started virtually from individual life.

Shila turns a person virtuous and for this reason Lord Buddha has laid so much stress on it. A virtuous person can exercise self-control and then as a key to all happiness and dedicated to goodness, one can reach to the entire depths of the nature of excellent conduct. He can progress on the path of salvation of self and then of entire universe.

In reality, one can start from self. By renunciation of evils, a person, while developing ideal virtues through his good deeds, leads on the path of self welfare and reaches the stage of salvation; establishes himself as ideal for others and then inspires others towards that path [of salvation]. An individual who is not able to proceed on the path of self-welfare and reach the ultimate can not become ideal or inspiration for others. This is the universal truth.

Beginning shall have to be made from the bottom; that is, from the level of individual.

This is the crux of teachings of *Hiinayaana*. It contains the condition of becoming light for welfare of self first. *Hiinayaana* message is to show enormous light to others after making the self luminous and shinning.

III

The *Hiinayaana* Buddhism is nucleus in the life of millions of people of the world in general and in Asia in particular. It is a matter of great satisfaction that people of a country like Thailand have assented Buddhism in their daily practices in the best possible manner through their casteless and equality-based societies and synthesizing culture, of which *Karuna*-the compassion, hospitality, sincerity, readiness towards self-reliance, development by peaceful means and hard-working temperament are the main features.

The five precepts[8], the three fold training[9], the law of action[10], four virtues[11] for a good or ideal household life[12] etc. are those great exemplary and emulative principles, which made the life of Buddhists worthy; they, side-by-side, give strengthen Buddhism to be followed by individuals and societies, even according to time and space.

Moreover, how to show respect to others' faith, ideas and views, can be learned from people of Buddhist countries, especially Thailand. Tolerance shown by people of Buddhist countries is exemplary; and this, as I believe, gives dimension, one after the other, to the development of their counties at various levels.

IV

Now, we are witnessing the days of unprecedented progress and globalization; these are the days of liberalization. World citizens are coming closer to one another in different walks of life. Day-by-day the tempo of mutual understanding and co-operation is increasing. We are continuously proceeding to become members of one and the same family by facing numerous problems and difficulties on our way. In such a situation, the way showed by Lord Buddha, or in other words, Buddhism, or the Buddhist teachings, especially pertaining to self-beginning are fully capable to become the basis of resolving all problems, from individual to international level, and to strengthen the spirit of global understanding and co-operation. More we come closer to them in our daily practices more we gain in the matter.

If *Karuna*-the compassion can be the best basis of co-operation and understanding at individual level, the

Panchasheela can be a solid basis of mutual relations, co-operation and understanding amongst the nations, societies and communities; also it can be the basis of resolving disputes-big or small, or of local to global level.

References:

1. Other three major religious communities are: Christianity, Islam and Hinduism.
2. Before Gautama Buddha, as the Buddhist treatises indicate, other Buddhas like **Dipankar**, **Mangal**, **Suman** and **Reot**, too, propounded the same philosophy in their respective ages.
3. *Atta Vaggo*-The Self, *Dhammapada*, Ch. 12, No. 116.
4. Of the *Dhammapada*.
5. Ibid. [*Aata Ha Ve Jitam Seyyo Yaa Chaayam Itaraa Pajaa, Aattadantassa Posassa Nichcham Sannotachaarino; Neva Devo Na Gandhabbo Na Maaro Saha Brahamana, Jitam Aapajitam Kayira Tathaarupassa Jantuno*]
6. [Aatanammeva Pathmam Pathirupe Nivesaye, Aathannamanusaaseyya Na Kilisseyya Pandito; Aattanache Tatha Kayiraa Yathannamanusaasati, Sudanto'vata Dammetha Aattaa'hi Kira Duddamo]
7. [*Attahi Attano Naatho Ko Hi Naatho Paro Siya, Attanaa' Va Sudanten Naatham Labhati Dullabham*].
8. *Panchasheela*.
9. *Triratna*.
10. *Karma*.
11. Four *Garavasa-Dharma*.
12. In this chain, four *Brahma Viharas* for social unity, ten principles [as duty] for a ruler and the Middle Path can also be mentioned.

Bibliography:

- Kumar, Ravindra [Ed.] Global-Peace-An International Journal, Volume 5, Number 4, September 2006
- Kumar, Ravindra, Towards Peace, Gyan Publishing House, New Delhi [India], 2006
- Max Muller, F., The *Dhammapada*, Atlantic, New Delhi [India], 1990
- Patyaiying, Paitoon, Thailand and the Asian Values, Krishna, Meerut [India] 2001

****

3

MAHATMA GANDHI

It was during my childhood that I had an opportunity to discuss a little about Mahatma Gandhi with my teacher for the first time. What conversation I had about is now lost in the abyss of time. But later I always wondered-why an international political leader like Gandhi was addressed as Mahatma, an honorific frequently used for a spiritually elevated soul. To find an answer, I think it is essential to review his life not in parts, but as a whole.

Gandhi affectionately called *Bapu* was a great leader endowed with a spiritual earning for truth. The quintessence of his philosophy of life was the realization of *Satya* [truth] and *Ahimsa* [non- violence]. His purpose of life was as he says:

"... To achieve self- realization, to see God face to face, to obtain Moksha [Salvation]."

But his approach was different from that of other seekers.

Gandhi received good *Samskaras* [pre-disposition] by virtue of his birth in a religious *Vaishnava* family of Gujarat, particularly from his mother who left an indelible impression of her saintliness on his tender mind.

He imbibed truthfulness from the characteristics of the hero of the play '*Harishchandra*'. He wondered:

"Why should not we be truthful like Harishchandra?"

The question haunted him day and night. The king Harishchandra became the ideal hero of his dream and the paragon of truth. He so inspired him as to remain truthful all through his life even under trying circumstances and stands firm on his convictions.

Gandhi's endeavours for self-realization were through strict observance of truth. He moulded his actions on the basis of truth, only the truth that he perceived within. The word truth ordinarily connotes not to tell lies. But for Gandhi it implied much more. Even hiding the truth from someone was deemed as untruth by him. He considered that the narrow implication of the term had belied its magnitude. Defining Truth he writes:

"The root of 'Satya' [truth] lies in 'Sat'. Sat means the 'Being' and Satya–the feeling of the 'Being'. Everything is perishable except 'Sat'. Therefore, the true name of God is 'Sat', thereby implying 'Satya [Truth] so, instead of saying 'God is Truth', it is better to say 'Truth is God".

A question may now arise whether the realization of Truth and the realization of '*Self*' were one and the same for him or the two entities. We get the answer from *Maharishi* Raman:

"What is Satya except self? Satya is that which is made of Sat. Again Sat is nothing but Self. So Gandhiji's Satya is only the Self."

It is now clear, what Gandhi meant by Truth was in fact the realization of Self. He writes:

" What I meant to achieve – what I have been striving and pining to achieve these thirty years – is self-realization, to see God face to face, to attain Moksha [salvation]."

How to realize God is a complicated question. The realization of God can be attained by purity of mind and heart and *Sadhana* [constant practice]. *Bhagvad-Gita*, the dialogue between Lord Krishna and Arjuna in the epic *Mahabharata*, is regarded as a sacred Hindu scripture and an infallible guide of daily practice. Lord Krishna tells about four paths of God-realization. They are the service and sacrifice [*Karma Yoga*], devotion and self- surrender [*Bhatia Yoga*], concentration and meditation [*Raja Yoga*], discrimination and wisdom [*Jnana Yoga*]. There is no line of demarcation between one and another and one path does not exclude the others. A seeker can follow any of them according to his/ her temperament. Ultimately they all lead to one goal – the realization of God.

Gandhi held *Bhagvad-Gita* in high esteem. He writes:

"Those who will meditate on Gita will derive fresh joy and new meanings from it everyday. There is no single spiritual tangle which the Gita cannot unravel."

He found answer to the above question in *Gita*–*Vairagya* [non- attachment] or *Abhyas Yoga* [practice]. *Vairagya* means total indifference to worldly things and concentration only on the Absolute. Lord Krishna says in *Gita*:

"Fix thy mind on Me only, place thy intellect in Me; then thou shalt no doubt live in Me alone hereafter."[1]

And further says he:

"If thou art not able to fix thy mind steadily on Me, then by Yoga of constant Practice [Abhyas Yoga] do thou seek to reach Me". [2]

Gandhi was born to serve humanity. He was a practical man; he chose the path of practice and the path of renunciation of the fruits of action. Absolute faith in God and surrender to His Will became his object of observance [*Niyam*] and the constant thought of the Truth – Practice [*Abhyas Yoga*]. His mind was always occupied with truth in all walks of life – personal, social or political.

Gandhi was a seeker and introspection was the method of his sadhna. He writes:

"I have gone through deep introspection, searched myself through and through, and examined and analyzed every psychological situation."[3]

The study of *Gita* and the process of self-introspection brought him face to face with the true meaning of *Ahimsa* [Non-Violence]–no violence in thought, speech and act. He came to the conclusion that the realization of Truth was impossible without adherence to the supreme conduct of man – *Ahimsa*. In his opinion Truth and *Ahimsa* were so inter- mingled as the two sides of a coin. For the achievement of one or the other, complete control over the senses of Action [*Karmendriya*] and those of Perception [*Jnanendriya*] is essential. Lord Krishna also says in *Gita*:

"Control Raga- dvesha [attachment–malevolence], obstructions on spiritual path; Do your duty well. Control desire and anger – the enemies of wisdom. Master first the senses. Kill this enemy - desire by restraining the self by self and by knowing Him who is superior to intellect".[4]

Truth and *Ahimsa* appear to be at the same level as a pair Truth – *Ahimsa*, yet Gandhi regarded *Ahimsa* as means [*Sadhna*] and Truth as the ultimate goal

[*Sadhya*]. It is said ahimsa is the super- most religion [*Ahimsa Parmodharmah*], Truth for Gandhi was the Almighty God. He, therefore, strived for and adhered to perfect Truth in thought, speech and act all through his life and thereby achieved the realization of self. It is most likely that he also practiced *Kriya Yoga* he was initiated in by *Paramhansa* Yogananda, who visited him in Wardha *Ashram* in 1935. Although lean and frail in appearance, he was strong in body and mind and glowed with spiritual health.

Gandhi once admitted that he had little knowledge of religions even of Hinduism, yet he believed, like every Hindu, in God, in rebirth and Salvation. He had a broad perception of Hinduism. In this perspective he says:

"I believe Hinduism is not an exclusive religion. In it there is room for the worship of all the prophets of the world. It is not a missionary religion in the ordinary sense of the term. It has no doubt absorbed many tribes in its fold, but the absorption has been of an evolutionary, imperceptible character. Hinduism tells each man to worship God according to his own faith or dharma and so live at peace with all religions." [5]

So, he regarded all religions with *Sambhaav* [equitability]. He perceived no religion was superior or inferior. He had studied about all religions of the world and came to the conclusion as he says:

"I believe the Bible, the Koran, and the Zend–Avesta to be as divinely inspired as the Vedas." [6]

He even tried in his mind to unify the teachings of the *Gita*, 'Sermon on the Mount' and the 'Light of Asia' and found Renunciation in *Gita* as '*the greatest philosophy of all religions*'.

Gandhi said:

"Nothing delights me as much as the music of the Gita or the Ramayana by Tulsidas." [7]

It will, therefore, not be out of context if we consider here the influence of *Ramayana* on him. *Ramayana* is an epic like Milton's '*Paradise Lost*' - a grand story, of a grand Man, in a grand style. But unlike '*Paradise Lost*', *Ramayana* is a sacred scripture of Hindus. Therein, Tulsidas has portrayed the persona magnum, Rama, as an incarnation of Vishnu as well as a model human being with high moral values to serve as example for common man. Frank Whaling writes:

"Rama has remained a symbol of dharma, human relationship and kingship; for others he has been a symbol of Brahman' or a symbol of the loving Lord." [8]

In his childhood, the repetition of '*Ramnaam*' [Rama's name] suggested to him to ward off his fear of ghosts and spirits became an infallible guide' for him later in life. Gandhi was highly impressed with the characteristics of Rama. Gandhi's heart was the permanent abode of Rama who was endowed with the attributes of *Brahmin*. Rama's obedience, ready submission to the vows of his father, his love for his subject, protection to the weak, and equanimity to all beings he met during his exile, left deep impressions on Gandhi's mind and heart. But what impressed him most was Rama's way of administration-*Ramarajya*, in which justice prevailed and the voice of the low of the lowest was given due respect. In fact, he regarded '*Ramarajya*' as the true model of democracy.

In introduction to his autobiography, Gandhi has written:

"My experiments in the political field are now known. But I should certainly like to narrate my experiments in the spiritual field, which are known only to me and from which I have derived such power as I possess for working in the political field." [9]

Indeed, he relentlessly pursued truth all through his life and achieved self-realization.

It is an anomaly that he is remembered and evaluated only for his political achievements. Little attention has been paid to the spiritual force within him from which he derived power to work in personal, social and political fields. According to *Maharshi* Raman, *Adhyatmik Shakti* [spiritual force] was working within him [Gandhi] and leading him on. He always listened to his inner voice and took decisions accordingly. His inner- self prompted him to serve the wounded in *Boer War* and *Zulu Rebellion* in South Africa. He was always in front line and fearlessly led people in *Satyagraha* and Non-Cooperation movements. Undaunted he walked unarmed without any protection through the riot- hit areas at the time of partition of India, giving message of faith, love and peace.

Gandhi was a *Yogi*-householder living amidst people. He was a *Nishkam Karmayogi* with no aspiration for any recognition or reward. He had limited his desires and needs to the bare minimum. Whatever he did, he did with right intention, right spirit and conviction, and worked for the benefit of others irrespective of caste, creed or religion. Notwithstanding the power he wielded over the Congress party and the masses, he never aspired for or accepted any kind of office. Had his name been proposed as the first President of India in recognition of his services to the nation, I am sure, none would have opposed it but he himself. He was such a great and magnanimous person. Rabindranath Tagore, a poet and visionary, recognized his greatness and spirituality and called him '*Mahatma*', an attribute he aptly deserved.

Lord Krishna says to Arjuna in Gita:

"Whenever righteousness declines and unrighteousness becomes powerful then I myself come to birth." [10]

If we turn to the pages of the history of the world, it is evident that there have descended super- beings whenever the righteousness or ethical values are on decline to guide people on to the righteous path. The Indian soil is credited with the birth of many a super-being or the lofty spiritual personages who inspired people to forsake the evils of materialism that cause suffering, dissatisfaction and misery and to follow the path of spiritualism. Rational explanations of Mahatma Gandhi's thoughts and acts will certainly place him in history in line with Lord Mahavira, Gautama Buddha and Jesus Christ. Gandhi stood for Truth, *Ahimsa*, Compassion and Service all through his life. 'To serve humanity is the service of God' was the principle of his life. He was a social saviour of the oppressed and down-trodden people and fought for their right of equality and justice. It is not all; he was the political saviour of nations in political turmoil. The leaders of many subjugated races and countries drew inspiration from him for their rights. Like Jesus Christ, he was Forgiveness personified. He had no feeling of malice towards anyone in his dying moments and breathed his last remembering his chosen deity 'Rama'. Paying a glowing tribute to Mahatma Gandhi, Albert Einstein has written:

> ***"Generations to come, it may be, will scarcely believe that such one as this ever in flesh and blood walked upon the earth."*** [11]

Today, we are passing through a crisis – a crisis of identification of values. The world is entrapped in gross materialism. Man has become as selfish as to have utter disregard for others whether an individual or a society or a nation. Scientists are vying with each other to play the role of the Creator. It is high time to create a balance between materialism and spiritualism. In the chaotic circumstances prevailing all over the world today, we are looking for peace as elusive as the mirage in a desert. I think that Mahatma Gandhi's life and his teachings can serve as beacon- lights to guide us and lead us to steady peace.

References:

1. Chapter XII: Shloka 8
2. Same as above, Shloka 9
3. Mahatma Gandhi in the Beginning of Twenty-First Century, page 20
4. Chapter III; *Shloka* 37 – 43
5. Mahatma Gandhi in the Beginning of Twenty-First Century, page 21
6. Same as above
7. Above
8. Gandhi and Gandhism, page 11
9. Mahatma Gandhi in the Beginning of Twenty-First Century, page 22
10. Chapter IV, *Shloka* 7
11. From Champaran to Quit India Movement, page

Bibliography:

- Gandhi, M. K., An Autobiography or the Story of My Experiments with Truth, Navajivan, Ahmedabad [India], 1957
- Gandhi, M. K., India of My Dreams, Navajivan, Ahmedabad [India], 1960
- Gandhi, M. K., *Sarvodaya*, Navajivan, Ahmedabad [India], 1955
- Gandhi, M. K., Young India, Ahmedabad [India], May 12, 1920, February 23, 1922 and December 20, 1928
- Kripalani, J. B., Gandhi: His Life and Thoughts, The Publications Division, New Delhi [India], 1991
- Kumar, Ravindra, From Champaran to Quit India Movement, Mittal Publications, New Delhi [India], 2002
- Kumar, Ravindra, Gandhi and Gandhism, World Peace Movement Trust, Meerut [India], 2001

- Kumar Ravindra, Mahatma Gandhi in the Beginning of Twenty-First Century, Gyan Publishing House, New Delhi [India], 2006
- *Shrimadbhagavad-Gita*, The *Bhaktivedanta* Book Trust, Mumbai [India], 1998

****

4

GANDHISM AND THE MODERN POLITY

Presently a big portion of the world happens to be under Democratic system of Government. Theoretically, this system stands out to be the best up to now. This is a truth. It is the best because people are connected with it directly or indirectly at every level. Not only this, it is this very system, which provides maximum opportunities of public progress and development. People can themselves decide in this system the mode of their welfare. However, even though being theoretically the best system of government, if we peruse the democratic nations, we first of all find that there is non-equal development of the citizens. We subsequently find that these nations are more or less victimized by regionalism. They have problem relating to language. They are under clutches of terrorism and communalism. There is also the problem of negation of human rights in these nations. There are other vivid problems akin to mention above and peace is far away so long as these problems exist. These nations should get themselves rid of these problems in toto, all citizens of them must have equal development and they should have communal harmony towards making all citizens collective and unified partners in progress. But, in reality, it is not so.

It is essential that the nations of democratic system of government should be free from above-mentioned problems, must be capable of ensuring equal development of their all citizens and the citizens concerned must march forward on path of progress in unified way along with rendering contribution to world peace. Gandhism is very much contextual today on this accord. It is significant. Let us grasp importance of Gandhism while analyzing it in brief.

GANDHISM

In quite simple and clear words, Gandhism consists of the ideas, which Mahatma Gandhi put forth before human world. Along with that, to the maximum possible extent, Mahatma Gandhi treated his individual life in accordance with these ideas. Clearly, Gandhism is a mixture of Gandhi's concepts and practices. I do not hold merely his theory to be Gandhism. The basic groundship of Gandhism happens to be non-violence.

The non-violence is the most ancient eternal value. This non-violence is the ground of ancient-most civilization and culture of India. Mahatma Gandhi said on this very account while making his concepts and practices based on non-violence:

"I have nothing new to teach you... Truth and non-violence are as old as hill."

As we know, non-violence and truth are two sides of the same coin. After knowing Gandhism, it is imperative for us to know clearly the concept of non-violence also as it accords the ground for Gandhism.

NON-VIOLENCE

What is non-violence? Ordinarily, we attribute non-violence as a dictum that prescribes non-snatching of anyone's life. Really, this is not complete derivation pertaining to the concept of non-violence. Non-violence is quite opposite to violence. As such, it would be better to know the position relating to violence in order to know non-violence and to be in knowledge of its meaning. According to a Jain scholar:

"Whenever, we hurt some other living being through our thought, utterance or action under non-cordial stipulation and non-apt learning, such an impure spirit or act of destroying life of some other one, including the impure tendency, utterance or presuming, is taken to be full of vice of violence. In such a situation, even if there is no sort of violence externally, it intrinsically ipso facto remains a tendency of violence."[1]

As a situation opposite to violence is non-violence, we can firmly state, ***"Total non-violence consists in not hurting some other one's intellect, speech or action per own thought, utterance or deeds and not to deprive some one of his life."*** We can clearly say this in a few words as follows: Abstinence in toto from violence is non-violence.

Mahatma Gandhi fully agrees with above-mentioned derivation of non-violence. He himself has said:

"Non-violence is not a concrete thing as it has generally been enunciated. Undoubtedly, it is a part of non-violence to abstain from hurting some living being, but it is only an iota pertaining to its identity. The principle of non-violence is shattered by every evil thought, false utterance, hate or wishing something bad unto some one. It is also shattered per possession of necessary worldly things."[2]

In this chain Mahatma Gandhi clarified in an edition of Young India:

"...To hurt some one, to think of some evil unto some one or to snatch one's life under anger or selfishness, is violence. In contrast, purest non-violence is epitome in having a tendency and

presuming towards spiritual or physical benefit unto every one without selfishness and with pure thought after cool and clear from the very beginning, there might have been self-doom by man".

However, it has not been that and not only human deliberations ***"... The ultimate yardstick of violence or non-violence is the spirit behind the action."***[3]

Mahatma Gandhi, while in principle admitting his concept of non-violence, clarified further in this respect and said:

[A] NON-VIOLENCE IS PERPETUAL

In context of non-violence being perpetual, Mahatma Gandhi states, ***"...When we peruse the era from beginning unto now relating to the period for which we gain historical evidence, we find that man has been ultimately treading path of non-violence".***[4] It is, as such, that non-violence came into existence along with man. In case it has not been with man from the very beginning, there might have been self-doom by man.[5]

However, it has not been that and not only human race is alive in such a huge number but there has been gradual enhancement in development and nearness in spite of presence of various obstacles and nuisances. This could never have been, but because non-violence is perpetual, it happened.

[B] NON-VIOLENCE AND TRUTH BOTH ARE COMPLEMENTARY TO EACH OTHER

Non-violence is governing because it is perpetual and permanent. It is on this accord that Mahatma Gandhi says, as I have already enunciated that ***"Truth and Non-violence are two sides of the same coin. Both have same value. Difference consists in approach only. On one side there is non-violence, on other side is truth".***[6]

The derivation is that Truth stays with permanence or that Truth is permanent. Non-violence on account of being permanently present stays to be true.

[C] NON-VIOLENCE AND COWARDICE UNRELATED

Mahatma Gandhi always believed in active non-violence. He had desisted inaction always like a brave man. It is a truth relating to non-violence that it is not a weapon of a week person. It has no place for cowardice. In own words of Mahatma Gandhi:

"...***Non-violence should not be mistaken to be a true battle against every sort of evil".***[7]

He further states:

"In contrast, non-violence of my conception is true battle against evil; it is active confrontation and not a device of tit for tat."[8]

Mahatma Gandhi clarified to those who were keen to take non-violence to be a weapon of the weak or those who terming it as concrete and was upbringing non-action:

"...Non-violence and cowardice are not at all inter-related. I can think of a person to be coward at heart even if he is totally armed. In case it is not taken as cowardice to be equipped with arms, it is certainly symbolical of fearfulness. Pure non-violence is impossible without pure bravery".[9]

He clearly said at innumerable occasions in time of national struggle for freedom that was being bravely carried out with fearlessness under his very leadership:

"...Non-violence is an active force. There is no possibility of cowardice or weakness in it".[10]

Further:

"There can be to hope of a violent person being non-violent one day but there cannot be such a hope in relation a coward".[11]

[D] NON-VIOLENCE IS SOCIAL AS WELL

Non-violence permanently exists in human nature and as I have stated, it came on earth with man. It can be said that one who is ***CREATOR*** of man on earth, is also ***ONE*** who kept non-violence permanently in human nature. Our existence could not have been if it was not so. We not only safeguarded our existence in its permanent presence but also progressed deeply and that is all clear before us. We are well aware that any progress is impossible without co-operation from others. When progress has been there, it is imperative that co-operation has been there. Co-operation is possible only when there is non-violence. As such, the non-violence, which is individually present, remains present socially also. It is in this accordance that Mahatma Gandhi says:

"...Non-violence is not only individualistic, it is social also".[12]

Logically, he further states in this regard:

"It must be developed. We are bound to admit that regulation of mutual relations in society is through non-violence to a considerable extent. I wish it to be developed on large scale".[13]

To those who take non-violence to be merely an individual notion, he said without mincing words:

"It is not true that society cannot be organized or operated on basis of non-violence. I oppose such a statement".[14]

[E] NON-VIOLENCE IS ALL-TIMELY AND ALL WELFARISTIC

As I have said, non-violence emerged on earth with man and Mahatma Gandhi took it to be perpetual and eternal. In this chain, he called upon the people to continue to develop it in practice throughout life while taking non-violence to be the basis of life. He said:

"Non-violence should not be practiced on specific occasion only".[15]

It is well timely. It is not short-lived or casual. Along with this, Mahatma Gandhi admits non-violence along with dogma of all-welfare and equality in toto. He separates it from utilitarianism completely and instantly from this point of view. In his own words:

"A so many times at a path but ultimately an occasion will be there when they will worshipper of non-violence cannot ditto utilitarianism. He will work towards 'Sarvabhoothitaya' that is maximum benefit of all and shall perish himself while constantly endeavouring to gain the ideal. Maximum pleasure of all includes maximum pleasure of maximum number also. Follower of non-violence and utilitarianism will be found find themselves forced to tread separate paths. In certain directions, they will also have to oppose each other. A utilitarian cannot sacrifice himself for the sake of saving his argumentation whereas a non-violent is always ready to face perishment".[16]

[F] GODLY FAITH IS ESSENTIAL FOR NON-VIOLENCE

Mahatma Gandhi integrally combines non-violence with God. According to him:

"It is impossible to tread path of 'Truth and Non violence' unless one has vital faith in God. God is that alive force which incorporates all remaining forces of the world. This force does not depend upon anyone and it exists even when all other forces in world come to an end. In case I do not believe unto this all glittering light, that incorporates everything, I fail to understand as to how am I alive!"[17]

God is really the Lord of universe. He accorded non-violence on earth along with man so that man can progress along with his existence and gain ambition. God kept all within the region of equality along with that. He has no consideration towards discrimination all small or big, high or low, rich or poor etc. It is possible only through developing non-violence that a man attempts to tread his life while practicing these non-discriminations in life. When man does so, he cannot at all ignore God who happens to be the Lord and who kept non-violence permanently in his nature.

These are some significant clarifications, which Mahatma Gandhi offers in context of non-violence. No doubt, non-violence is natural, true, and perpetual and a device that is far away from cowardice. It is social value also along with being an individualistic one; it is all-timely and all welfaristic. It is essential to believe in God if one cherishes to believe and practice non-violence. When I myself ponder over, I firmly believe that all eternal values get themselves comprehended unto non-violence. Forbearance can be there only while non-violence is in existence. Unity, compassion, fraternity, justice or equality is also for its help alone. It is basis, mother and up bringer of all the values.

MAHATMA GANDHI, NON-VIOLENCE AND DEMOCRACY

While accepting dictum of all-welfare as basis and not that of majority, [18] Mahatma Gandhi is certainly a staunch supporter of democracy and along with that, he wants that it should be intermingled with non-violence in every manner. In such a democracy:

"Quantum of interference in liberty of people happens to be the minimum".[19]

In fact, Mahatma Gandhi takes real democracy to be that admits governmental interference at the minimum, which has peace at the maximum and all progress on the basis of equality. It is possible only when non-violence is imparted the supreme status in practice as well as in principle and at social as well as individual plane. Only such a democracy can be successful in its real goal.

We could know the derivation pertaining to non-violence and also by perusing Gandhian point of view, its significance for human race. We could clearly know that it is only non-violence, which can make life prosperous at every level. When it is so why should not the democratic countries make themselves prone to non-violence in the event that these countries with democratic governance system accept welfare of all citizens to be their ambition or goal? Mahatma Gandhi wants this very all out of the system of government and it is really a thing of significance. It is such a significant matter that this reality cannot be denied by me or by anyone amongst you. It is on this accord that Gandhian non-violence is immensely significant in system of today's governance, especially in a democratic system.

Presently, the democratic system in operation in worldly nations is not according to Gandhian principle. We are not getting what Mahatma Gandhi ultimately cherished from democracy. If it was so, these nations could be devoid of atmosphere of violence and presence of fear.[20]

There could not have been corruption and divided human society. I have already emphasized that there could not have been problems pertaining to terrorism, communalism, regionalism and problems relating to languages. More than this all, there could not have been observance of ethical and moral degradation in public life. Such degradation is being observed constantly. The main cause after all these things remain that all activities of these nations are not non-violent. There cannot be any possibility of violence while there is Gandhism in democracy. Violence is not sacred, pure or welfaristic from any point of view. Whatever is gained on basis of it is impure and temporary. It is on this accord that it cannot pace with democracy even for a moment. Mahatma Gandhi says: ***"Democracy and violence can never be mutual".*** [21]

Basis of democracy is non-violence in toto. And, there cannot be any diminution in it. Non-violence should be real; not merely titular. Democracy shall be pro-people only while so. Mahatma Gandhi said in this context:

"If they are to be truly made democratic, they must be valiantly non-violent". [22]

In case of absence of this attribute, democracy shall be there for name sake only and it would be better for it to... clearly be supporter of dictatorship. [23]

MODERN SYSTEM OF GOVERNANCE AND NON-VIOLENT GANDHIAN WAY

After above-mentioned analysis, the question arises before us as to how to guide modern system of government, especially democracy, towards Gandhian way, which undoubtedly has non-violence as its basic root. Then, it is to be made and quotable towards equal development of all citizens. This democracy must be such that ***"it should not warrant power of punishment".***[24]

In it, ***"... people will certainly be conscious regarding their duties: they may sometimes, of course, be ignorant towards their rights".***[25]

In case there is something anti-people in it, the people shall make it favourable to them through non-violent means.

As we have analyzed, Mahatma Gandhi is in favour of spontaneous development of non-violence. To make democracy ultimately in accordance with non-violence remains to be his goal. This is possible. He rightly said in this regard, ***"... Non-violence is not merely an individual concept. It is social concept also. It must be developed in this form".***[26]

Development is essential and it is in sight. He again states in this regard along with citing a nice example:

"Mutual practices in society are regulated by non-violence to a considerable extent. I want it to be at development at larger scale".[27]

This should of course, be done in right direction and with truthful spirit. It is the inference that the non-violence permanently present in human nature should be developed in practice from its present state towards progressive one in right direction per truthful spirit. A true and cherished democracy shall be established only in such a condition. A system shall be commendable in proportion to non-violence in it. This is important regarding every system, however, the government of the people-democracy-remains foremost in this chain. We have accordingly assigned it topmost place under our discourse.

Polity must be fearless, full of equality, providing protection to all eternal values and only then it can be pro-people. It can accord apt dimension to development. Man can contribute to world peace only in such a system of government along with gaining his goal. Government should be welfaristic to people and above being non-violent as enunciated by Mahatma Gandhi. Gandhian principle of non-violence is very much significant in modern system of government from this point of view. This significance is likely to be of permanent nature perpetually.

THE DEMOCRACY OF MAHATMA GANDHI'S IMAGINATION

Yes, the democracy of Mahatma Gandhi's imagination-fully encircled with non-violence -exists in no nation of the world as up to now. Democracy of his imagination happens to be one, which does not have any provision of punishment and even an organization like 'State' happens to be obsolete in it. This is because Mahatma Gandhi holds, ***"...State is symbolical of centralized and organized violence".***[28]

As non-violence is connected with human soul, man can be non-violent whereas in opposition to it, ***"... State is a soul-less machine. On this accord, it is impossible to get rid of violence. Its very existence depends upon violence".***[29]

Non-existence of state as cherished by Mahatma Gandhi is impossible instantly or in near future. Even then, it is incumbent on the people, who are living in state organizations, to develop non-violence that is permanently present in their nature and to enhance it gradually up to adequate level. Along with that, all systems [specifically democracy] should, work in direction of development of non-violence at individual, community, social and national levels. The atmosphere of fear which we see, the diminution of values in life and the problems having cropped up vividly cannot be eradicated without developing it.

There is no alternative to non-violence. The whole human history is within our purview. Whenever polities were under clutches of violence, tacitly or expressively, they could not get anything except doom and disaster to their citizens. Their own peace was fully shattered per this doom and others were also badly affected. It is in this regard that in accordance with philosophy of Mahatma Gandhi, non-violence should be admitted as invariable part of our life and it is on the basis of this dictum that modem polities must operate. This will be very nice for them.

I have stated that polities cannot all of a sudden operate as per expectation of the Great Mahatma Gandhi. Non-violence cannot be a part of conduct instantly, but Mahatma Gandhi's suggestion is very important in this regard[30] as I have already mentioned. However, the polities must forward certainly in this direction. Needless to say that non-violence is true, natural, and enemy of fearfulness, stands at top amongst eternal values including the equality and has been gradually progressive. Its nice and vital example is before us in the form of its development unto today, since the inception of human race-that is since initial human-state. We clearly see that in spite of differences to whatsoever extent, ultimately there is an innovative desire for peace. This is because non-violence happens to be in human nature, as I have said time and again, human being like it.

Gandhism calls upon modem polities to march in this direction and to make them prone to non-violence. This is really welfaristic. We cannot at all minimize significance of Gandhian non-violence in modem polity.

References:

1. *Jain Darshan*...page 321
2. *Mangal Prabhat*, 1945, page 7
3. Young India, October 4, 1928
4. *Harijan Sewak*, August 11, 1940
5. Young India, January 2, 1930
6. *Harijan Sewak*, July 13, 1947
7. Young India, June 4, 1925
8. As Above.
9. *Harijan*, July 15, 1939
10. Young India, June 16, 1927
11. As Above.
12. *Harijan*, July 1, 1939
13. As Above.
14. Above, December 3, 1939
15. Above, September 5, 1936
16. *Sarvodaya*, 1955, page 4; Navajivan [Hindi], December 1, 1926
17. *Harijan Sewak*, July 28, 1946
18. On March 2, 1922, Mahatma Gandhi clearly wrote in the Young India, ***"It is slavery to accept every decision of majority. Democracy is not an epitome in which people should behave like sheep. Liberty of man's thoughts and actions is cautiously guarded in Democracy."***
19. *Harijan,* January 11, 1936
20. The notions having democratic system are practically the victims of difficulties and problems even though they are committed to total and equal progress of their citizens. People in general are not fearless and their life is far away from peace.
21. *Harijan Sewak,* November 12, 1938

22. As Above.
23. Above.
24. The Epic Fast, 1932, Page 102
25. *Harijan*, March 15, 1938
26. As Above, January 7, 1939
27. Above.
28. Modern Review, 1935, Page 412
29. As Above.
30. *Mahatma Gandhi says*, **"My opinion rests on my belief in the infinite possibilities of the individual to develop non-violence. The more you develop it in your being, the more infectious it becomes, till it overwhelms your surroundings and by and by might over sweep the world."** [Mahatma- D. G. Tendulkar, Volume 5, 1952, page 14].

Bibliography:

- An Autobiography or the Story of My Experiments with Truth, Navajivan, Ahmedabad [India], 1957
- Gandhi, M. K., [Ed.], *Harijan* Weekly [Files till 1948], Navajivan, Ahmedabad [India]
- Gandhi, M. K., [Ed.], *Harijan* Sewak Weekly [Files till 1948]
- Gandhi, M. K., India of My Dreams, Navajivan, Ahmedabad [India], 1960
- Gandhi, M. K., *Sarvodaya*, Navajivan, Ahmedabad [India], 1955
- Gandhi, M. K., [Ed.], Young India Weekly [Files 1919-31], Navajivan, Ahmedabad [India]
- Manjushri, Sadhavi, Jaina Philosophy and...Aditya Publications, Delhi [India], 1992
- Shastri, Manoharmuni, *Isibhasiyain Suttain*, SGM, Bombay [India], 1963

****

5

GANDHISM TODAY

Mahatma Gandhi, an apostle of peace was a votary of 'Truth' and 'Non-Violence'. For him the two are essential for each other. In other words '*Truth*' and '*Non-Violence*' cannot set apart from each other. They are two sides of the same coin.[1] 'Truth', which, according to Mahatma Gandhi, is God[2], is the ultimate goal of life and '*Non-Violence*' its means. Contrary to the view that spirituality comes from the scope of mysticism, Mahatma Gandhi believes that it is fully under the scope of ethics. As opposed to many scholars and intellectuals of the day, especially from the West, for him to lead a spiritual and religious life mean the same as to lead a selfless ethical life full of '*Love*' and '*Non-Violence*' constitutes the essence of ethics. For Mahatma Gandhi to realize '*God*', or '*Truth*', or '*Self*' or '*Moksha*' or '*Mukti*' or '*Vimukti*'-the liberation means the same as to realize a perfect enlightened and selfless life of love.

Mahatma Gandhi realizes that a liberated human life is eternally the best form of life. Peace and happiness, which involve in a liberated life, are not only everlasting but also of the highest degree. Any person can pursue '*Truth*'- the ultimate goal of life, through selfless service to ones society to the best of ones ability and making constant effort to purify ones inner world. He realizes that such a life involves leading a life of selfless service to society, to the best of one's ability, through some division of work required for common good, which constitutes the foundation of *Varnashrama Dharma*-system in ancient India. But he firmly rejects the present caste system, which divides the Indian Society in 3500-4000 parts and sub-parts, as it is, according to him, the antithesis of the *Varnashrama* and the sooner people abolishes it the better.

For Mahatma Gandhi, to acquire spiritual knowledge is not to acquire knowledge through some extraordinary perception about some mystical entity called the '*Soul*' or the '*Self*', but to acquire knowledge with the help of reason based on one's spiritual experiences about the distinction between the life of selfless love and the life of selfishness, and the means to spiritual perfection from the life of selfishness. He is of the opinion that religious knowledge as well as ethical knowledge is empirical scientific knowledge. Also he was of the opinion that the man who discovered for us the '*Law of Love*' was a far greater scientist than any of the modern scientists. He believes that modern science is replete with illustrations of seemingly impossible having become possible within living memory. But the victories of physical science would be nothing against the victory of the '*Science of Life*', which is summed up in love-the Law of our '*Being*'. Thus Mahatma Gandhi can be regarded as the apostle of the scientific religious life of his age.

Although Mahatma Gandhi has not authored any book on theory of human life but his thoughts on various aspects of human life provide a systematic understanding on the subject, which is essentially the same as the understanding of human life of great ancient and contemporary teachers and seers. The great teachers and seers of ancient Indian Civilization had a common, deep, comprehensive and scientific understanding of human life, although they had differences in the realm of metaphysics. Even now, through their great teachings, they guide us to a true, comprehensive and scientific theory of the distinction between spiritual and non-spiritual life. Along with this, they provide the means to transform a non-spiritual life into an enlightened, perfect and spiritual life. Mahatma Gandhi has admitted that our tradition has been swept by many evils such as casteism, gender-injustice etc., and he consider it to be our supreme duty to make systematic efforts to root them out.

Mahatma Gandhi believed in fundamental ethical unity and truth of all religious communities. He admitted that the basic values of all religious communities[3] were the same and true; and that inter-religious dialogue would be conducive to lasting inter-religious harmony. He admitted that he believed in the fundamental truth of all religious communities of the world. He also believed that if all could read the scriptures of different faiths from the stand points of the followers of those faiths they must find that they were at bottom all one and were all helpful to one another.

He was of the firm opinion that India has the moral and spiritual resources to provide a welfaristic culture of '*Truth*' and '*Non-Violence*' to the whole world, when in technological age all religious communities could grow harmoniously in spite of their differences in the realm of metaphysics.

Today under the spell of the modern view, especially of the West, the ethics is not considered a scientific study. It is not an essential part of syllabus even in India. Mahatma Gandhi firmly believes that study of ethics should be introduced[4] right from the beginning of educational curricula. According to him, ethics forms the foundation of building of good character and healthy society. He has said that a child before it begins to write its alphabet and to gain worldly knowledge should know what the '*Soul*' is, what '*Truth*' is, what '*Love*' is? Along with this, a child should learn that in unavoidable struggle of life he must gain victory over hate through love, untruth through truth and himsa-violence through ahimsa-non-violence and self-suffering.

In his work, *Hind Swarajya*, Mahatma Gandhi made a severe condemnation of the Western Civilization of the day and articulated an alternative involving retelling the basic values of the great teachers and seers of ancient Indian Civilization in the context of present technological age. It was his firm opinion that in the materialization of his vision lay the true freedom of India, and through India of the world at large. He considered Western Civilization of his time to be essentially an irreligious and false one in the sense that selfless ethical love that constitutes the essence of religious life has no place or only peripheral place in it, and what it considers to be the ultimate goal of life is essentially false. It fails to look at not only the true value of spirituality, i.e. of selfless ethical love for human being but also the truth about many traditional and eternal ethical principles such as Non-violence to all life, non-slavery to passions and senses, abstention from avarice, contentment, external and internal purity, body-labour, non-adultery, etc., which all great religious philosophies and seers accept to be eternal and ethical principles. The followers of the so-called Modern Civilization explicitly reject many of these eternal ethical values and do not even take note of some others. Mahatma Gandhi did not change his view about Modern Civilization, especially the Western Civilization, till the end of his life.

Contrary to the belief, Mahatma Gandhi was not against machinery; however, he was against the replacement of *Shareershram* [body-labour] by machine work. Side by side, he was not against making physical work more joyful with the help of the machines. Simultaneously, he believed that willing obedience to the law of body-labour could bring contentment and health. He would certainly oppose that Western form of development that has caused the disappearance of thousands of plant and animal species, resulting in greater damage to the nature sustaining life and health, but he would not be against development based on the principle of Non-violence. He was not against the pursuit of wealth and pleasure within the bounds of ethics.

Mahatma Gandhi supported neither a blind rejection of the Western Civilization of the day nor a blind acceptance of traditional Civilization of India. He wrote that there was nothing to prevent him from profiting by the light that might come from the West. Only he must take care that he was not overpowered by the glamour of the West. He must not mistake the glamour for the light.

As the basic values of all religious communities are the same, the rejection of the Gandhian alternative to Modern Civilization, especially of the West, means the rejection of the fundamental values of all great religious communities. Today the basic values of the great Indian

Civilization are being affected. It is a matter of serious concern that the welfaristic values of the great Indian Civilization and are continuously disappearing from our day-to-day practices. The temptation of the glamour of the Modern Civilization of the West is becoming too strong to resist. Let us make an in-depth and critical analysis of the Gandhian approach as an alternative and take initiative for a national debate on it at the earliest possible. Definitely, it will be a real tribute to the legacy of the Great Mahatma, the apostle of peace and a votary '*Truth*' and '*Non-Violence*'.

References:

1. *Harijan Sewak*, July 13, 1947
2. In his autobiography- My Experiments with Truth, Mahatma Gandhi admits, ***"My uniform experience has convinced me that there is no other God than Truth"***
3. Including Hindu, Sikh and others
4. Essentially considering it as one of the four pillars of the system

Bibliography:

- Gandhi, M. K., An Autobiography or the Story of My Experiments with Truth, Navajivan, Ahmedabad [India], 1957
- Gandhi, M. K., *Harijan Sewak* [Hindi] Weekly, Navajivan, Ahmedabad [India], July 13, 1947

****

6

GANDHI AND VALUE EDUCATION

Mahatma Gandhi's name requires no introduction because of his invaluable contribution to the national liberation movement of India. It was he who awakening crores of people on the strength of non-violent activities, engaging them to an action, challenging the mighty empire of the world, ultimately threw the yoke of slavery. Those who believed that not a single country in the world history had achieved its freedom except by violent means, the action of Mahatma Gandhi compelled them to re-think and also to change their mentality. His reputation as a true nationalist as well as an internationalist shines like sun itself, but in the academic sense of term, he is not considered a great scholar or an educationist. We have not been enlightened by his views on education or on the problems relating to it, through any particular book written by him. Even there is no special research article available, which could have given us a glimpse of his ideas or suggestions on education system, except his occasional articles on the future of education in India written in a very simple and light manner. The same thing applies to the views he expressed on the subject now and then.

Despite this fact, the few articles that Mahatma Gandhi has written in the simplest manner, and the views he expressed on education as a common man are of utmost importance; they provide us a guide line to proceed towards value education. Not only this, if we apply them even in the modern perspective, they can, definitely, give a new dimension to our education system.

Mahatma Gandhi once said:

"Education means all-round drawing out of the best in child and man – body, mind and spirit."

As such, education becomes the basis of personality development on all dimensions – moral, mental and emotional. Therefore, we can say that in the long run education forms the foundations on which the castles of peace and prosperity can be built. Since ancient times, it is said '*SA VIDYA YA VIMUKTAYE*', which means that with education we finally attain salvation. This small Samskrit phrase essentially contains the thought and essence of Value Education that is relevant in all perspectives. This very concept, when applied to the simple but refined approach of Mahatma Gandhi, can provide us with a new dimension of educational development. As such, while analyzing the views of Mahatma Gandhi, we can observe his views under two main points:

A. MORALITY AND ETHICS

Moral and ethical knowledge is the first point on which Mahatma Gandhi's concept of value education is based. Any education system that lacks these two cannot be termed as good. The reason behind such a thought is that, without morality and without ethics, no student, in real sense, can be considered to be healthy in mental and physical terms, because for it, self-control and good character is essential. A person, who is not a moralist and who does not differentiate between right and wrong, cannot rise to the essential level of a true student. Then, the attainment of spiritual growth that has been described by Mahatma Gandhi, as an essential part of education, can only be gained through morality and ethics. Seeing it through another viewpoint also proves the same thing because when we consider education as a means of attaining salvation and also as a support on the pathway to liberation, then we cannot differentiate it from spiritualism.

Mahatma Gandhi laid down some rules for students so as to ensure that morality and righteousness always be considered as an essential and un- differentiable part of education so that every student shall gain in terms of knowledge and spirituality. He said that on one hand where students should gain education under the strict regimen of high morals, self-control and right thinking, on the other they would also be expected to provide service to the society in general. This includes their respect towards mother, father, teachers and elders, adorations towards younger, following of social traditions and constant awareness towards their duties and responsibilities.

In order to strengthen morality and ethics in students, Mahatma Gandhi advocated the introduction of religious education. This kind of education brings the values of forbearance, tolerance and reverence in one's character. And in turn, these values are an indivisible part of ethics. Explaining the importance and need of religious education, Mahatma Gandhi writes in the 'Young India' of 6th of December 1923:

"A curriculum of religious instructions should include a study of the tenets of faiths other than one's own. For this purpose the students should be trained to cultivate the habit of understanding and appreciating the doctrine of various great religions of the world in a spirit of reverence and broad minded tolerance." [1]

Mahatma Gandhi calls upon all teachers to impart proper education of morality and ethics to students both at school and college levels. In this regard suggesting some guidelines for teachers, he says that it is the duty of teachers to develop high morals and strong character of their students. If teachers fail to do so, it means that they depart from their social and national responsibilities and as such they are also insincere towards their noble profession. He said that a teacher should lay an example, to be followed, before society and students. This can only be done when he himself leads his life with high standards of morality and strong character. An ideal teacher should be free from any addiction. He needs to be polite and should set an ideal example of simple living and high thinking. He should also remember that wasting time is a sin; therefore, he should be aware of his duties towards students and society. Moreover, he should have a good reputation in the society. Therefore, it is the foremost duty of students, as well as of teachers to make it certain that moral and ethical knowledge continues to be the integral part of the education process. By doing so, they can contribute in the development of Value Education.

B. *BUNIYADI* [BASIC], JOB-ORIENTED OR TECHNICAL EDUCATION

Another important point of Mahatma Gandhi's value education is basic or technical education. No matter if the word '*Buniyadi*' [or basic], which Mahatma Gandhi used during the 3rd and 4th decade of 20eth century, meant the knowledge or education that could help rural people in promotion of village handicrafts or to establish cottage industries, the ultimate purpose behind his attempt was to make young men and women self-reliant in the economic field.

Even in modern perspective, his idea of '*Buniyadi*' or basic education is well-worthy and it has no clash with the concept of today's job-oriented or technical education.

In fact, Mahatma Gandhi wants to prepare a student for technical knowledge right from the days of his primary level of education. In this regard, his logic is not only important but adaptable; it can prove to be a mile stone in the direction of value education. I myself, too, have the same kind of viewpoint already elaborated in some of my articles. [2]

It is not so that Mahatma Gandhi has not talked of all-round or complete education on different occasions. He definitely spoke of imparting education based on curriculum; he, more or less wrote about graduate and post graduate levels of education. Not only this, as I have just discussed, he laid emphasis on moral and ethical knowledge, which is helpful for character building and for the physical and mental development of a student since the very beginning of his education. He clearly believed that without a healthy body, mind could not be developed fully. But even after that he, without any hesitation, said that until and unless education makes a young man or woman self-reliant, it is of no value.

It is but obvious that when a child starts his formal education, he enters at primary level and, step by step, at an age of twenty or twenty-two, he graduates from a University. And after so many years, if he does not find a necessary goal or if he lacks a direction to begin with his career, then what could be the use of such education. What is the use of the degree for him that he has in his hand?

Reality lies in the fact that after obtaining a degree the students should definitely have a clear direction for their future; they should have no doubt towards their future goal. They should be full of self-confidence. Side by side, they should be self-dependent and capable to tackle unavoidable day to day problems. They must not be worried for a suitable job.

But in reality, these days we see that our younger generation is directionless. Our youths are diverted and a feeling of helplessness and dejection is prevailing on them. According to a survey, there are millions of men and women who, even after completing their studies at graduation, post graduation and doctorate levels, fail to seek an employment of their choice. Is it not a failure of our social and educational system?

Even after spending the golden years of one's life in attaining higher education, our youths are not self-dependant. As such how would they be able to get rid of their day to day problems and how would they contribute to their society and the nation? Therefore, it is a challenge not only before the youths of this country but also before the educationists, scholars and those in the government.

To tackle this problematic challenge, Mahatma Gandhi's views can be of great support. In this reference, he has given us his golden words that there is a need of result-oriented education. He said that every child has some special qualities that can also be termed as inherited traits of personality, so at the very primary level, a student's quality and worth should be identified by his teacher. A student should gain education according to curriculum and moral guidance and as such also improve his physical strength. But the teacher should watch and identify his quality that could be of help in his later life.

For that purpose it is necessary that after completing studies to a certain level, he must, in addition to above three kind of education-general [according to syllabi], moral and physical- be provided facilities to gain technical knowledge in accordance with the special trait that has already been identified in his personality by his teacher. Since by nature he has interest in that knowledge, he will easily gain it; he will become an adept in that. Now, when he completes his study up to graduate level and with this extra knowledge comes out of a college or university, he would have a direction. As such, even if he does not get a private or government job, he would manage to get through some sort of self-employment on the basis of his technical knowledge. At least, then, his education would be considered as result-oriented.

This indeed is Mahatma Gandhi's view-point pertaining to Value Education if applied in a wider perspective. Its worth lies in the fact that education should necessarily be helpful in employment and its foundations should be laid on morality and ethics. We all who are concerned with it need to think over it deeply. We have to apply Mahatma Gandhi's ideas according to present circumstances of our country and also as the demand of time. I can again say that Mahatma Gandhi's unique and refined views about value education are not only important but are worth applying not only in India but also in the rest of the world.

References:

1. In this regard further he pointed out, ***"This, if properly done, would help to give them a spiritual assurance and a better appreciation of their own religion...There is one rule, however, which should always be kept in mind while studying all great religions and that is, that one should study them only through the writings of known votaries of the respective religions."***

2. In one of my articles entitled, ***"Education in the Twenty-First Century: Problems and Expectations"***, written in 1997 for the Golden Jubilee Souvenir of the University of Guwahati, Assam [India], I have mentioned two examples to clarify my view-point.

Bibliography:

- Gandhi, M. K., [Ed.], *Harijan* Weekly, Navajivan, Ahmedabad [India], March 3, 1935, May 8, 1937, July 31, 1937, August 28, 1937, September 11, 1937, October 9, 1937, April 4, 1940, March 23, 1947
- Gandhi, M. K., [Ed.], Young India Weekly, Navajivan, Ahmedabad [India], September 1, 1921, August 25, 1927, August 2, 27 and December 12, 1928

****

7

GANDHI AND HIGHER EDUCATION

Mahatma Gandhi in his article titled '*National Education*' published in Young India on 1 September, 1921 has written that it might be true regarding other countries but in India where eighty of the population is occupied with agriculture and 10% of it with industries, it is an offence to make education merely literary[1].

It is apparent from these lines that according to Mahatma Gandhi, education is not limited to gain literary knowledge. Although he has tried to confine his above mentioned statement within the Indian perspective, in my opinion education cannot be restricted to the knowledge of letters of alphabet or the study of literature irrespective of the circumstances or the economic resources of any nation in the world. In addition to the literary knowledge, education includes the moral, physical and mental development of a person.

In course of time, education has to develop a person in all respects in order to enable him to become self-reliant. A man cannot make an all-round progress or cannot be self-dependent on the basis of any of the qualities of intellect, and physical or spiritual development. To become self-dependant or for his all-round development, it is necessary that he should have moral upliftment in addition to his physical or intellectual development. It is absolutely necessary that he should not only be able to earn his bread, but should be able to fulfill the obligations of his family and carving the path of his progress should ultimately be able to achieve his goal of life.

A young man or a young woman may pass the Graduate or the Post-graduate examination with first division or may further acquire the M. Phil. or Ph. D. degree, but still he/she does not become self-dependant and is not able to canalize his/her future along successful lines by worrying out his/her day-to-day problems. In such a case, will the education received by him/her or the degrees acquired by him/her be regarded as meaningful? In my opinion such an education or such a degree is useless. Probably, you also will regard such education incomplete. It is the reality that can be perceived not only in India but in other countries also. Therefore, Mahatma Gandhi's statement that education does not mean getting literary knowledge is entirely true even in the context of the world.

Today, there is a large crowd and a lot of competition for getting admission in colleges and universities. It is very true in the case of higher education.

Everyone wants to go in for graduation, post-graduation, M. Phil or a Ph. D. degree. It is not all; thousands of students stand in a queue for D. Lit. degree. What prospects are there after getting a degree or degrees? Many of them have no hope for a bright future. Now you tell me, a person, who has spent a major, precious part of his life in obtaining a degree or passing through any level of higher education and who has not received any guidance for future or is unable to make himself self-dependant, should be considered educated? The answer would be in the negative. It is happening so. It appears that education today has failed in giving any direction.

It is a fact that our system of education has been defective for the last many decades. Even after independence, our leaders have not taken such steps as they should have to reform our defective educational system. Since independence and till now, many committees have been constituted, many commissions have been formed, but how much improvement has been made in the sphere of education? Not much. People like Dr. S. Radhakrishnan and Dr. Zakir Hussain, the well-known educationists on national and international levels, have been the Presidents of our country. It is an anomaly that education has not been able to give right direction to our youths, or to provide them opportunities for their all-round development or to make them self-dependant. The number of students for higher education has increased every year and is still growing further. If we do not awake in time and bring changes in our defective educational system according to the view-points of Mahatma Gandhi, the situation would become so serious that we would not be able to manage it.

Mahatma Gandhi, an advocate of a solid foundation for the human beings was firm on giving free and compulsory elementary education[2] to all. In Harijan of 9 October, 1937, he wrote that he was firmly in favour of the principle of free and compulsory education for India. He further wrote that at this level along with the training in any trade, their physical, mental and spiritual potentialities also be developed. Under present circumstances, I would like to add further that arrangements should be made for free and compulsory education to all up to the secondary level[3] without any discrimination of lineage, gender, creed, caste or sub-caste. The government should do this. I firmly believe that if Mahatma Gandhi had been with us today, he would have held the same opinion.

It is also to be arranged to impart physical and mental training for the growth of good physique and mind and moral education for the formation of character and good conduct on the elementary and the secondary levels. Besides, students should have technical knowledge according to their interest at these levels so that it may enable them to become self-dependant in future. This type of education imparted at the secondary level will incorporate four kinds of education, viz. technical, physical-mental, moral and general [according to syllabus]. After having received the secondary education, the students would certainly become self-dependant and would be able to choose the career they would like to follow.

Each and every student should have a definite aim before he enters the field of higher education; otherwise it is meaningless to pursue higher education. There is general thinking today that they would decide what they would do after having passed B. A. or M. A. or acquired some other degree. It is sheer waste of time and money and they would not achieve anything except groping in the dark. They will have a clear-direction only when the system of education at the secondary level is managed on the lines I have briefly discussed. Regarding this, it can be further said that a student should primarily pursue his studies at graduate level on the basis of the elementary technical education he/she received at the secondary level along with the other three. It is the requirement of the nation and is important at international level as well. There is also the possibility of their becoming self-dependant. If Mahatma Gandhi's views on higher education are analyzed and reviewed in the perspective of the circumstances prevailing today, the above stated educational system would be according to them. It will be in proximity to his statement by which he expressed his desire that by changing the nature of college education, he would make it conform to the needs of the nation.[4]

Having become a graduate with technical knowledge any young boy or girl would be capable of seeking self-employment in a country with large population as India and it will be comparably easy for him/her to get a government or non-government job. He or she can also pursue his or her studies further while doing his/her job. In this way, being self-dependant, a young boy/girl can continue his/her studies further to fulfil his/her aim and object. This is what Gandhi wanted. Contrary to it one who is self-employed will not have to run about after graduation for post-graduation or any other higher degree. Apart from this, he will not be required to waste his precious time and money. It will naturally bring down the unnecessary crowd in colleges and universities. Besides, education will be purposeful and will be able to guide in right direction. In short, these are Mahatma Gandhi's views on higher education and keeping them in mind, the system of education in India will have to be reformed. Mahatma Gandhi's these views can be our guide and can contribute to the management of our educational system.

Mahatma Gandhi had talked about self-sufficiency of colleges and universities. It meant that these institutions instead of depending on the government-aid should be self-financed. India is an agricultural country. Most of the industries are based on agriculture. Gandhi wanted that more and more self-financed Agriculture-Colleges should be opened and they should be attached to related industries which would turn out graduates according to their requirement. Not only this, they should bear the expenses of their education and the training-staff. Gandhi wanted the same system to be adopted for the engineering or medical graduates. The engineering graduates should be attached to the related industry and the medical graduates to hospitals. The Law, Commerce and Arts colleges can be managed by the voluntary organizations and donations can be procured according to their requirement. Mahatma Gandhi was never in favour of government-aid. He, however, wanted the universities' control over the colleges and that of the government over the universities.

It is another matter that under the present circumstances, we have not been able to incorporate his views in our system of higher education, but they are worth giving a thought. The self-dependence he has talked about is certainly significant, otherwise how long will the colleges and the universities thrive on government-aid? Keeping it in view, we will have to make a firm and well planned schedule and put it into practice.

Reference:

1. Mahatma Gandhi's article titled, *'National Education'* is not only the best for solving the then problems pertaining to education, but many of its parts are relevant even today.
2. Up to standard VIII.
3. Up to standard XII.
4. *Harijan*, July 31, 1937.

Bibliography:

- Gandhi, M. K., [Ed.], *Harijan Weekly*, Navajivan, Ahmedabad [India], July 31 and October 2, 1937, November 11, 1947
- Gandhi, M. K., [Ed.], Young India Weekly, Navajivan, Ahmedabad [India], August 6, 1925
- Kumar, Ravindra, Essays on Gandhism and Peace, Krishna, Meerut [India], 1999

****

8

GANDHI AND PEACE EDUCATION

Gandhism, in quite simple and clear words, is an amalgam of Mahatma Gandhi's views and practices. In other words, it consists of the ideas which Mahatma Gandhi put before the world, and side by side, to the maximum possible extent, treated his individual life in accordance with these ideas. Those who hold merely his theory to be the Gandhism, they are not correct, because simply his theory cannot be accepted as Gandhism.

Gandhism revolves around *Ahimsa*-non-violence[1], which is the most ancient, perpetual, individual as well as social, all timely and welfaristic value; it is an active force, connected with God and, thus, stays to be true, and it is a *Dharma* in grandeur.[2] Along with this, non-violence is permanently present in human nature, and it is an essential condition for existence, the basis for development and the achievement of the goal.

Now, what is the goal? From both, the spiritual and social, point of view, it is peace. Peace is a purpose behind the creation[3] for all most all, whether atheists or theists. And it is because of this, emphasis has been laid on the continuing awakening and adoption of non-violence, individually and collectively in our day-to-day practices.

Not only by Tirthankara Mahavira, in whom manifestation of *Ahimsa*-the non-violence took place in the best possible manner[4], or the Buddha and Mahatma Gandhi[5], but also by other apostles of peace, philosophers and thinkers of the East and the West made efforts for the construction of a culture accepting non-violence to be the fundamental point so that the existence of mankind is assured, the path of development is smoothened and the ultimate goal is well within sight and approach. There is no let-up in these endeavours; and this process shall continue with the same gusto in future as well.

History of mankind which is very old, running into millions of years and divided in different ages, proves the fact, time and again, that among all other beings only man has the quality of intellect and creativity. And it is due to this that he has been able to pass through the process of leaning by doing, or in other words, especially from Gandhian point of view, the real education, which played a very vital role and made a sizeable contribution in awakening of non-violence and its application in daily practices, whatsoever method may have been adopted with the changed times. It was necessary from the point of view of those who define education as '*Sa Vidyaya Vimuktey*.' [6]

As the whole world knows, in this very chain, in the 20eth century, Mahatma Gandhi made a momentous contribution showing a wonderful, simple and justifiable way for awaking and practicing of non-violence in the routine chores of life. When I say the above way of Mahatma Gandhi to be wonderful, simple and justifiable, it is because Mahatma Gandhi, by establishing co-ordination and synthesis between all concepts of the East and the West, old and new, makes non-violence well worthy to be grasped by all. Everyone can, more or less, find non-violence of his imagination in Gandhi's principle pertaining to it, and also in his practices, and it is only the great characteristic of his non-violence and due to this it is unique as also of special recognition.

To make non-violence the basis of maximum day-to-day practices of man, Mahatma Gandhi, right from the beginning considered it to be an indivisible, important and essential part of education. Development of morality and ethics in a man since his childhood, by imparting moral and ethical education, right from his primary studies, is the most important step in this regard; as it is the first of the four pillars[7] of that educational plan which I have tried to propose and is necessary for all round-development of personality in general and to proceed on the way to peace in particular. Also it is one of the two aspects[8] of that unique and refined approach of Mahatma Gandhi, pertaining to value education, which provides us with a new dimension of development in the matter.

And that's why an education system that lack these two-morality and ethics- cannot be termed as good and complete in its term and objective. The reason behind such a thought is that without morality and without ethics, no student, or in later stage a man, in a real sense, can be considered to be healthy in both, the mental and physical, terms, because for it, self-control and good character is essential. A person who is not a moralist, and who does not differentiate between rights and wrong, cannot rise to the essential level of true student, and who does not rise to this level, he surely cannot contribute towards the development of the culture of peace.

In fact, for construction of a culture of peace the attainment of spiritual growth, that has been described by Mahatma Gandhi as an essential part of education, can be gained only through morality and ethics. Seeing it through another viewpoint also proves the same thing, because when we consider education as a means of attaining salvation and also as a support on the pathway to complete peace, the liberation, we cannot differentiate it from spiritualism. And it is for this reason that Gandhism also laid down some rules for students so as to ensure that morality and righteousness always be considered as an essential and un-differentiable part of their education, and they gain in terms of knowledge and spirituality. In this regard he clearly mentioned that, on the one hand, where students should gain education under the strict regimen of high morals-self-control and right thinking; on the other they should also be expected to provide service to the society in general that includes their respect toward mother, father, teachers, and others, adoration towards younger, and following of social traditions and constant awareness towards their duties and responsibilities.

The purpose behind Mahatma Gandhi's advocacy of the introduction of religious studies in education can also be seen in his intention to strengthen morality and ethics in students. This kind of education brings the values of forbearance, tolerance, and reverence in one's character. And, in tern, these values are supplementary to and within the domain of great value of *Ahimsa*-the non-violence. In this very context, explaining the importance and need of religious education, Mahatma Gandhi even went to the extent in one of the issues of Young India:

"A curriculum of religious instructions should include a study of the tenets of faiths other than one's own. For this purpose the students should be trained to cultivate the habit of understanding and appreciating the doctrine of various great religions of the world in a spirit of reverence and broad minded tolerance."

Although to make it sure that moral and ethical education is imparted to students, and later it has permanent place in men, Mahatma Gandhi fixed responsibility of each and every concerned individual, whether parents, teachers, leaders of society, student or a man himself, but he especially called upon all teachers to impart proper knowledge of morality and ethics to students at the primary, secondary and higher level of education.

In this regard suggesting some guidelines for teachers, he said that it is the duty of teachers to develop high morals and strong character of their students. If teachers fail to do so, it means that they depart from their social and national responsibility and, as such, they are also insincere towards their noble profession. He said that a teacher should lay an example, to be followed, before society and students. This can only be done when he himself leads his life with high standards of morality and strong character. An ideal teacher should be free from any addiction. He needs to be polite and should set an ideal example of simple living and high thinking. He should also remember that wasting time is a sin; therefore, he should be aware of his duties towards students and society. Moreover, he should have a good reputation in the society from moral and ethical point of view.

Along with teachers he called upon students and said that it would be their foremost duty to make it certain that moral and ethical knowledge continues to be the integral part of education process. By doing so, they can contribute to the development of value education that is essential for building of an ideal peaceful and prosperous society. Simultaneously, he equally emphasized on its continuation after finishing formal education, and called upon each and every one to acknowledge it till the last breath of life.

The other aspect of Gandhian approach relating to value education is also important for construction of a sustainable culture of peace. This aspect is basic or technical education, no matter if the word *Buniyadi* [or basic] which Mahatma Gandhi used in the third and the fourth decades of the twentieth century meant the knowledge or education that could help people in the promotion of handicrafts or to establish cottage industries. As the ultimate purpose behind his thoughts and attempt was to make young men and women self-reliant in the economic field, even in the modern perspective, his idea of *Buniyadi* or basic education is well-worthy, it has no clash with the concept of today's job-oriented or technical education; it make a man self-dependent and prosperous. No doubt, a self-reliant and prosperous person can, definitely, contribute towards peace and prosperity of society and the nation and can equally be helpful to create a stable and real culture of peace.

Mahatma Gandhi did this, so that every human being living on this planet, without fear, and equally marching towards development process, was assured of safe and secure life having peace, and strengthening the culture of peace.

In fact, Gandhism and its system of education, especially its viewpoint pertaining to value education is, ultimately, the education of peace and to make a man fully developed, and it is according to Mahatma Gandhi, ***"is an unending process divided into different stages..."*** Its worth lies in the fact that education should necessarily be helpful to make a man self-dependent and its foundations should be laid on sound morality and ethics.

It is, undoubtedly, ever relevant for achieving the goal-peace-or for construction of a real and sustainable culture of peace, especially under the democratic system of government. In this context its relevance and importance of its role can never be underrated. It should be applied in wider perspective. The need of the day is to take up, adopt and understand Gandhian approach according to time and space and to put it into practice in the process of education the world over. Indeed it is the demand of time.

References:

1. Although abstinence in toto from violence is non-violence; or consisting of not hurting some other one's thought, utterance and deeds by one's own thought, utterance and deeds, and not to deprive a living being of his life, is non-violence, but regarding the acid test, necessary for non-violence, Mahatma Gandhi's argument 'that the ultimate yardstick of violence and non-violence is the intention behind the action', deserves due consideration.
2. In all of its meaning whether adoption of good, or duty or the way of life.
3. In case we accept the view that there is no purpose behind creation [of human being], our life become simply meaningless. That's why we must accept the idea of purposefulness, no matter if we are atheists or theists.
9. Young India, 6 December 1923. Be it the Buddha or *Tirthankara* Mahavira, Lord Jesus Christ or Prophet Muhammad, everyone was of the singular opinion that there was a purpose behind creation of mankind of mankind.
4. Who declares it to be the soul-force.
5. Who, ultimately, accepts it to be a natural-value.
6. Meaning thereby, education makes capable of liberation.
7. The other three are: General [according to prescribed syllabus], physical and technical [*Buniyadi*].
8. Another one is basic [*Buniyadi* or technical] education.

Bibliography:

1. Fischer, Louis, Gandhi: His Life and Message for the World, New American Library, New York, U. S. A., 1954
2. Gandhi, M. K., *Harijan* Weekly, Ahmedabad, India, 15 July 1939; 30 September 1939; 6 July 1940

3. Gandhi, M. K., Yong India, Weekly, Ahmedabad, India, 6 December 1923 and 4 October 1928
4. Green, Martin, Tolstoy and Gandhi, Men of Peace: A Biography, Basic Books, New York, U. S. A., 1983
5. Kumar, Ravindra, Essays on Gandhism and Peace, Krishna, Meerut, India, 1999
6. Kumar, Ravindra, Mahatma Gandhi at the Close of Twentieth Century, Anmol, New Delhi, India, 2004
7. Kumar, Ravindra, Theory and Practice of Gandhian Non-Violence, Mittal, New Delhi, India, 2001
8. Tendulkar, D. G., Mahatma: Life of Mohandas Karamchand Gandhi, Volume 5, V. K. Jhaveri & D. G. Tendulkar, Bombay, India, 1952
9. Tolstoy, Leo, The Law of Violence and the Law of Love, The Unicorn Press, London, U. K., 1959

****

9

GANDHI AND INDIAN CULTURE

Speaking in a conference at Allahabad on April 5, 1936, Mahatma Gandhi said about India Culture:

"Many of us are striving to produce a blend of all the cultures which seems today to be in clash with one another. No culture can live if it attempts to be exclusive. There is no such thing as pure Aryan Culture in existence in India Today. Whether the Aryans were indigenous to India or were unwelcome intruders, does not interest me much. What does interest me is the fact that my remote ancestors blended with one another with the utmost freedom and we of the present generation are result of that blend."

Gandhi's above statement with special reference to the Indian Culture is extraordinary and factual, though at the first glance, it may appear general and ordinary. Extraordinary it is for the reason that Gandhi has said a lot in brief for the simple reason that this statement would be of great help, to some extent if we intend to explore the main features of the Indian Culture.

The first most important point about the culture that Gandhi has brought out in this statement is that any culture that tries to remain exclusive cannot survive. It means that for the long life of a culture, it has to remove rigidity and avoid parochialism. The rigidity and parochialism are in fact two demerits which keep one isolated from others and ultimately prove themselves self-defeating or in other words result in self-destruction. As opposed to it, flexibility and liberality are the two attributes that bring on synthesis and continuity in life. They function as a force of unification and not of segregation. It is necessary here to clarify while talking about flexibility; I do not mean that we have to break loose from all constraints and to refrain from being firm. Though the Indian Culture is known for its liberal and magnanimous attitude, it has never deviated from its fundamental values. This is the reason that it is still alive even after a lapse of thousands of years whereas, the other cultures about which we study in history are now non-existent. The main reasons for their disappearance are those that I have enumerated above.

In the perspective of Indian Culture, the second important point which Gandhi has raised is that there is nothing like pure Aryan Culture in the country. Discarding the concept of Aryan and non-Aryan cultures as unimportant issue, he says that our ancestors mingled with each other so well that the outcome is the present day generation. It clearly shows that Gandhi has on one hand struck at fundamentalism and on the other has brought out the basic principle of harmony. It is evident from history that the Indian Culture many a time was subjected to fundamentalism, but it could not deviate from its basic principles of patience, tolerance and above all non-violence. Sometimes it appeared that Indian Culture would lose its form because of fundamentalism and other attacking forces, but it did not happen and the culture remained firm on its course of progress. Consequently, the fundamentalism and the other weakening forces proved to be momentary and disappeared like water-bubbles.

Synthesis is a significant feature of the Indian Culture. We can also say that is the basic principle of the culture, the history of which goes back to the ancient past or we can certainly line it up at least with the *Dravidian* era. Later on, many other cultures came in contact with the Indian Culture and easily merged themselves into it according to the circumstances and conditions that prevailed in India rather than those in the land of their origin. In the same context, Gandhi is very true when he says:

"It [Indian Culture] nurtured the synthesis of those cultures which stayed in this country. They affected the Indian way of life and in return got influenced by it."[1]

Continuing further Gandhi regarded the homogeneity of the Indian environment the basis of this synthesis.

History is witness to the fact that all those cultures that came in contact with the Indian Culture were not completely or partially devoured by it. Not only did the Indian Culture through its great values make am impact on other cultures, it also imbibed their befitting features. This is the reason that there was no possibility of any pretence of harmonious blending of cultures. There was not anything forced upon, nor was their existence ever questioned. After the synthesis of *Aryan* and *Dravidian* cultures the vast Indian Culture came to be viewed in its entirety by the people of the world. Later on, many other cultural streams that flowed into the Sub-Continent from Greece, Persia, Arab countries or any other parts of Europe merged themselves into the vast ocean of Indian Culture. If we put aside the question of how and why these cultures arrived in this country, the picture that emerges before us reflects the unique characteristic of synthesis of Indian Culture.

It is fact that the Indian Culture is grand and unique and has fostered other cultures. Gandhi, in his time, was a great exponent and representative of Indian Culture. We can call him an embodiment of Indian cultural heritage glimpse of which we can have in his brief statement on Indian Culture exposing its characteristics of magnanimity, flexibility and above all of synthesis. Whatever views

Gandhi held on Indian Culture and spoke about, he himself acted accordingly. He occupied himself with re-establishing the genuine cultural values throughout his life. As he has himself affirmed in the opening lines of his statement, he has in principle and practice remained firm on his views:

***"To remain aloof from the rest of the world or do erect walls around us...it is [definitely] to go astray."*[12]**

It means that to keep ourselves with in the confines of narrow-mindedness and rigidity is to get lost and ultimately lose our entity. To do so will also be against the everlasting and coordinating culture of India which is replete with non-violence and its supplementary values such as patience, tolerance and progressiveness. Therefore, he urged his colleagues and the countrymen to act upon the real cultural values, but prior to it, he advised them to assimilate them.

Gandhi was justified in his grievance that the prosperous Indian Culture in which there is no alternative to the great values it represents, has not been given due recognition, made a subject of study and the specific features of which have not been properly evaluated. It is not all; he was unhappy with the disregard for it and the indifference to its values in their day to day application.

Hence, in one of the issues of Young India, he wrote, ***"Our culture is a treasure-house of such great values as are hardly found in other cultures. We have not given it its due recognition; have seen it and learnt about it by not conducting ourselves according to its tenets; [but] without the conduct, more disregarding its proper study and undermining its values. We have almost discarded it intellectual knowledge is just like a corpse that may be preserved as mummy. It seems good to look at, but fails to inspire."*** It means to observe the characteristics of a culture in right perspective and to comport oneself accordingly. It is does not happen so, in his own words, ***"...will be like a mass suicide."***

Gandhi's views as a representative of Indian Culture are founded on facts, for they present it in right perspective; they make him an embodiment of cultural heritage. In brief, these views along with his conduct conforming to them will always remain capable of guiding one and all who would work with a desire to keep the true Indian Culture alive. It is not all; they will also be a source of inspiration to all other cultures of the world for their longevity.

References:

1. Young India, November 17, 1920
2. As Above, September 1, 1921

Bibliography:

- Gandhi, M. K., *Harijan* Weekly, Navajivan, Ahmedabad [India], May 9, 1936
- Gandhi, M. K., Young India Weekly, Navajivan, Ahmedabad [India] November 17, 1920, September 1 and 21, 1921
- Kapp , K. W., Hindu Culture and Economic Development, A. P.H., Delhi [India], 1963
- Kumar, Ravindra, Education, Culture and Civilization, Krishna, Meerut [India], 1999
- Kumar, Ravindra Five Thousand Year of India Culture, Dynamic Publications, Meerut [India], 2003
- Vivekananda, Swami, Caste, Culture and Socialism, Advaita Ashram, Calcutta [India], 1965

****

10

NON-VIOLENCE

Non-violence, that is *Ahimsa*, is not a rough thing, nor is it an inactive thought or a value established by man. Non-violence is a natural, dynamic, active or live value. Because of its permanent existence in human nature, its being dynamic and active non-violence is an essential condition for existence, development and the ultimate goal, and for this very reason it is the first and absolutely necessary base of civilization.

Best manifestation of non-violence took place in Lord Mahavira. For Mahavira non-violence is the soul-force. Besides being nucleus in Jain philosophy, the form of non-violence that shaped in his individual practices and daily routine, nevertheless, it did not exist in the life of any of his contemporaries. It this regard Mahavira is unparallel even today; and after him anybody equaled him or has been able to follow him completely, is beyond my knowledge and belief.

Further for Gautama Buddha, and in modern times, for Mahatma Gandhi, non-violence is, ultimately, a natural value. As for many incarnations, prophets, philosophers and thinkers, since ancient to modern times, for Buddha and Gandhi also it is the principal human value. Although

Gautama Buddha did not directly accept the naturalness of non-violence, but the manner in which he has repeated love for life as innate desire by all [*Sabbes Jeeviyam Piyam*], and disliking for violence and punishment [*Sabbe Tashanta Dandassa*], the conclusion is drawn that non-violence is a natural value. Buddha laid stress on maximum purity in daily practices and he called for practical non-violence as much as possible. For this reason, non-violence became the subject of more and more practices in his philosophy.

Mahatma Gandhi's arguments that "***man has made consistence progress in direction of non-violence***" and in a natural way "***mankind moved towards non-violence for progresses***" spontaneously confirm the naturalness of this value from his side also. For Gandhi too, non-violence is the subject of maximum practices and ultimately its yardstick is the intention behind the action. According to Mahatma Gandhi, importance lies in making non-violence conducive to circumstances of time and space; it is the base on which success of non-violence depends. No doubt, this conception towards non-violence is acceptable to all-general or particular.

Non-violence of Mahavira is the soul-force whereas non-violence of Buddha and Gandhi is a natural value. By speaking so, readers may presume that there is a difference in views of Mahavira, Buddha or Gandhi regarding non-violence. In other words, there is a difference between above-mentioned concepts relating to non-violence in which it soul-force according to Mahavira, while it is a natural value according to Buddha and Gandhi. But in reality it is not so. Definitely soul reflects the nature, or we can say that nature is influenced by soul. Therefore, the one that is the soul-force is, more or less, natural also.

So far as the question of non-violence being dynamic and live or an active value is concerned, in that Mahavira, Buddha, Gandhi and many other also, are unanimous. Let us now have some discussion regarding non-violence being a dynamic and active value.

As historical evidences confirm, in its primitive age man adopted the technique of living and stabilizing together. By doing so, man showed co-operation towards fellow man, which, like affection, is another supplementary value of non-violence. And interestingly, even in primitive age, after mutual co-operation humans did not make a final stop. Man did not stop satisfied at the feeling of his own safety and that of his contemporaries. On the contrary he had a keen desire to move forward. In other words, man was crazy enough to further develop the sense of mutual co-operation. And this was the reason that he continuously co-operated with others and established new records, one after the other. Because of this natural instinct man is still on the path of progress and he has to go further and further. Despite the presence of many hurdles, worldly competitions and envy, the instinct of co-operation with others could not elope from human nature and it will never elope. Because of this instinct man will remain active as far as possible, he shall continue to proceed towards prosperity.

Not on the strength of any theory, but on the basis of day-to-day practices and self-experiences, any one can reach the conclusion that non-violence and non-violent activities, and mainly co-operation, increases further with more efforts; it becomes conducive to us. Therefore, it can be emphatically said that non-violence is dynamic besides being an active value. Needless to say that non-violence is in our nature and it has the capacity to consistently develop. Any one who has least doubt in the activeness of non-violence or its dynamism, he can remove doubt by experiences of worldly practices of his own and others. There can be no question mark on non-violence being an active, dynamic and natural value.

Natural, active and dynamic value non-violence is entirely linked to heroism, or in other words, heroism is a necessary condition for it, and also an acid test of non-violence. There is no correlation between non-violence and cowardice. *Vardhamana* became *Veera* [the brave] on the strength of non-violence and he became '*Mahavira*' by adopting it his life.

Non-violence has the power which cannot be conquered by anyone. In the time of Buddha, Angulimal, who wore garland of fingers extracted from the bodies of people killed by him, once faced Buddha. Gautama Buddha was passing on his way when Angulimal came in front of him and he challenged Buddha to change his route, but Buddha did not care for his challenge. He was an apostle of compassion [the *Karuna*] and compassion is the best supplementary value of non-violence. In this way, even being full of compassion, Buddha was definitely a brave also. Why should he be afraid of Angulimal? Buddha went on walking and at one time both were in front of each other. Buddha stood before him with strait eyes, but Angulimal could not see eye-to-eye; he got defeated and became Buddha's follower. This was the strength of non-violence.

Many more such examples can be cited, but here I will discuss only one example more, which is related to Mahatma Gandhi and then give full stop to my talk. It was the month of March in the year 1930. Mahatma Gandhi was proceeding towards Dandi from his *Sabarmati Ashram* of Ahmedabad. A man of a place near Bharoach, who was opposed to the principle of Gandhi, threatened him to kill in a lonely place. Anyhow, Gandhi got the news.

He was a worshipper of non-violence and, therefore, fearless and brave also. He knew that anyone having ill-will cannot withstand before the power of non-violence. Two-three days passed. In the meantime Gandhi got ascertained the name and address of that ill-willing person and one day, in early hours, he confronted him. Gandhi told the man, "***Brother! I am Gandhi; you want my life. Take it soon, none will know.***" The man could not see eye to eye with the votary of non-violence and became his follower. This is the reality of natural, dynamic and active or live value non-violence and of non-violent hero.

Bibliography:

- Gallie, W. B., Philosophers of Peace and War, Cambridge University Press [U. K.] , 1978
- Gandhi, M. K., *Harijan*, Ahmedabad [India], September 5, 1936
- Gandhi, M. K., India of My Dreams, Navajivan, Ahmedabad [India], 1960
- Gandhi, M. K., Young India, Ahmedabad [India],
- Gregg B., The Power of Non-Violence, James and Clark, London [U. K.], 1960
- Jacobi, Herman and Max Muller, F., Jaina Sutras, Volume I, Atlantic, New Delhi [India], 1990
- Kumar, Ravindra, Fundamentals of Civilization, Gyan Publishing House, New Delhi [India], 2006
- Kumar Ravindra, Gandhian Thoughts: An Overview, Gyan Publishing House, New Delhi [India], 2006
- Kumar, Ravindra, Non-Violence and its Philosophy, Dynamic Publications, Meerut [India], 2003

- Kumar, Ravindra, *Shanti Ki Aur*, Volume 1 & 2, Love & Co., Meerut [India], 2001-2002
- Manu, *Manusmriti*, Randhir, Hardwar [India], 1992
- Manjushri, Sadhavi, Jaina Philosophy and... Aditya Publications, Delhi [India], 1992
- McAllister, P., Reweaving the Web of Life: Feminism and Non-Violence, New Society, Philadelphia, Pennsylvania [U. S. A.], 1982
- Miller, William Robert, Non-Violence: A Christian Interpretation, Schoken Books, New York [U. S. A.], 1964
- Muni, Madhukar, *Aacharanagsutra*, I & II, APS, Byavar, Rajasthan [India], 1980
- Rajneesh, Acharya, Philosophy of Non-Violence, Motilal Banarsidas, Delhi [India], 1964

****

11

MORALITY

A review of thousands of years of human history, in which various civilizations raised their flags in different parts of the globe, from time to time, confirms the fact that morality always remained established in human society in both forms, direct as well as indirect. Morality, as one of the strong supplementary value of non-violence, not only existed, rather it functioned as a guide remaining active and dynamic in daily chores of man; and ultimately it called for all-round human welfare and inspired man for this purpose.

Since morality remained dedicated to human welfare, and played important role in making and unmaking of various civilizations, it is necessary that we should get introduced to the meaning of morality.

In India, from very ancient times, consistently and under all circumstances, the message was for progress and welfare of all, general and particular; and while doing so, it was declared that ***"this is the highest moral law" and if "we all adopt this live truth, all laws relating to morality will themselves appear."***

According to *Bhagvad-Gita* morality is a part of duty. But of which duty! Generally of the same duty, under which actions for prosperity of all are accomplished without any self interest, without any desire or expectation of reward and by dedicating to that symbol of oneness, the God. No doubt, this is a repeat of message of human welfare in the *Gita*.

In Indian philosophy morality has also been treated as *dharma*. By doing so, it has been said:

"In real terms man can be called moralist, or in other words dharmic [religious], if he is above hate and selfishness, whose life is perfectly pure and who is involved in service of all. Only such a person can best perform for humanity; and truthfulness is the basis of all this best and highest."

All important concepts regarding dharma, like ***"adoption of goodness or the best"*** or ***"discharge of ones duty"*** are incorporated in this declaration. Not only had this, a scholar, while expressing his views regarding relationship of dharma and morality, has even said:

"If we loose the morality like base in our life, without any doubt we get separated from dharma." According to this scholar, ***"There are no religious discourses that are not moral. For example, a person,***

who talks of torture and repression, and act untruthfully, he cannot claim to be following the path of God."

Clearly, here the good deeds also become the acid test of morality. Such deeds become worth following for others, besides individual welfare of man.

All principles and practices of Mahatma Gandhi have been full of morality. Let us see what he says about morality. At one place he says:

"True morality does not lie in following the path of defeating others, rather to search the path of truth for self and in fearlessly following it." In this very context, at another place Gandhi says, "In fact, the life of a moralist is full of virtues, or in other words, he leads a life full of virtues and that too, not for the reason that by doing so he is benefited, rather because this is the law of his existence; definitely it is the base of breath. In very brief we can say that virtue itself is the reward of man."

After all here we have discussed about noble deeds; they are made the basis of morality, and it is dedicated to welfare of all. *Dharma* [whether adopting goodness or discharging duties or in whatever context] is bound by it and the path of truth passes through the domain of morality. In simplest language, or speaking clearly and also in brief, morality is the best manifestation of true virtues, with which duty is inseparably linked, and saying again, its objective is the welfare of all.

Above-described meaning, explanation and objective of morality is not confined only to Indian concept; scholars, philosophers and thinkers from the West, who have spoken or written about morality, more or less, agree to this meaning, explanation and objective. In this context, first of all, let us talk of German scholar G. F. Nikolai. According to him:

"There is no logical system behind the concept of moral feeling, rather it is natural disposition inherited from [ones] ancestors."

In the explanation of Nikolai, thus, there are three dimensions about morality:

It is a naturally developed sentiment;

It is linked to duty and is a subject of '*action*' not of '*logic*'; and

It is in competition with immoral deeds.

According to another German scholar Martin Nimular, all, general and particular, should follow the life style and ideals of Jesus Christ and practice them in their life; life and deeds of Christ were the climax of morality. Simultaneously, many other thinkers of the West have, more or less, expressed the same views, and not only in the philosophy of modern thinkers, but they are found in messages of ancient thinkers like Socrates also.

Ultimately, views of both, the West and the East, about morality are almost similar. Both are near to each other. Let us think, if Nikolai treats morality as natural, and by linking it with duties, find it involved in competition with immorality, where is it against the concept of morality defined in *Shrimadbhagavad-Gita*, Vedas or by great man like Mahatma Gandhi? Side by side, if Martin makes Christ, whose life and deeds were dedicated to welfare of all, as the base of his principle of morality, where is the difference between his concept and the concept of the East, and especially India? Not only this, in my own view, even social thinkers like Bernard, who suggests two separate concepts of morality for man and woman, are not out of the above field.

Bibliography:

- Dasgupta, Subbhayu, Hindu Ethics and the Challenge of Change, Arnold-Heinemann, Calcutta [India], 1977
- Gandhi, M. K., India of My Dreams, Navajivan, Ahmedabad [India], 1960
- Gratisayanski, P. S. and Others, History of Political Doctrines, Part 1 to 4, Progress Publications, Moscow [U. S. S. R.], 1976-89

- Kumar, Ravindra, Fundamentals of Civilization, Gyan Publishing House, New Delhi [India], 2006
- Kane, Pandurang, History of the Dharmashastra, Part 1 to 5, Hindi Samitee, U. P., Lucknow [India], 1973-80
- *Shrimadbhagavad-Gita*, The *Bhaktivedanta* Book Trust, Mumbai [India], 1998
- Sogani, Kamalchand, Ethical Doctrines in India, J. S. S. S., Solapur [India], 1967
- Vivekananda, Swami, Modern India, Advaita Ashram, Calcutta [India], 1963

****

12

REVERENCE FOR LIFE

It has been depicted, most beautifully and clearly, in the first line of a *Shloka* of *Jinavangmaya* that '*SAVVESI JIVIAM PIYAM*', i.e., life is dear to all. Every living being, to a very intense and significant extent, has the will to live. This is a desire which manifest itself. A living being wishes to live so long as he can. Any person, sentenced to capital punishment if asked suddenly to choose one betwixt *Nav-Nidhi* [the nine treasures] and life, he will choose life. When it is established that all living being want to live and no one has accorded us a right to kill, there should not be any attempt to kill any one. No one should be tormented. In case we cause to pain to some one, try to strike and injure or try to take some one's life, some or the other will also try to take revenge upon us. This is the very stage to start animosity and hostility. Hence, it is incumbent upon us that we respect the right of lives of all.

The second line of this *Shloka* states '*PANINCHA PIYA DAYA*', i.e., all living beings cherishes mercy or pity in the same direction as they dislike attack on life. Suppose there are two people standing at a place before an animal. One of them holds a knife in his hand and the other a bunch of grass. Seeing both, even the animal's eyes make it clear that the man with grass in hand is only acceptable to it. So, to give protection to all living beings should be an attitude of man. It should be remembered that one who protects others and has the tendency of *Daya*, he himself becomes fearless. Thereafter he has generally no fear from any person. As such protection is the most important aspect of life. So it has been very rightly said that among all the charities, protection to life is the best.

The third line has the reference that '*ATMAVAT SARVABHUTESHU*', i.e., always keeping in minds *AHO ATMAN* meaning thereby, to consider all living beings as ones' own self. To have a feeling of pain/sorrow for all beings of the world, keeping in mind that the affliction is being caused to us, the pain will be suffered by us as by others. While doing so, the last line of the *Shloka* directs, '*PARASPAROPGRIGO JIVANAN*' which means a person should contribute good will and co-operation to a great extent. The creativity of the creature consists in the fact that he mutually co-operates. It is the only condition to make life worth-living.

At the root of all the above four lines flows the current of non-violence, which gives the great message of harmony in the best possible manner, having regard for all lives. This, in fact, is the only welfaristic way for ones own self and equally for others. The concept of reverence for all lives and their protection is relevant and cannot be refuted because only through it anyone and everyone, keeping their lives safe and protected, can proceed towards the goal. Come! Let us continuously advance in this direction.

Bibliography:

- Horney, Karen, Our Inner Conflicts, W. W. Norton, New York [U. S. A.], 1945
- Jacobi, Herman and Max Muller, F., Jaina Sutras, Volume I, Atlantic, New Delhi [India], 1990
- Kumar, Ravindra, Essays on Gandhism and Peace, Krishna, Meerut [India] 1999
- Kumar, Ravindra, Religion and World Peace, Sara Publications, Meerut [India], 1997
- Mehta, Mohanlal, *Jaina* Philosophy, Sanmati Gyanpeeth, Agra [India], 1959
- Shastri, Devendramuni, Jainachara..., S. S., Udaipur, Rajasthan [India], 1982
- Shastri, Kailashchand, Jainadharma, B.D.J. S., Mathura [India], 1966

****

13

SUFISM IN INDIA

Since ancient times, people have tried to solve the mystery of life. Through the ages, this curiosity made people to experiment with things and know the hidden forces behind their actions. This has given rise to the system of science, which has made astounding discoveries and advancements over the past century. But, for every moment, life declares itself to be something fuller than a blind play of physical forces, however complex and sublimated their interactions are. Scientists explain it in their own way but science only describes life, it cannot feel it.

There is a special form of craving - the craving for the Infinite. It is a state when people cannot find rest except in communion with a Supreme Reality free from all imperfections and limitations; and such a Reality can be found in nothing less than the Unconditioned Absolute.

C. G. Jung, the famous psychoanalyst, once said:

"Among my patients from many countries, all of them educated persons, there is a considerable number who came to see me, not because they were

suffering from a neurosis, but because they could find no meaning of life..."

This is the point where people start thinking beyond science. They wish to know the unknown forces that drive all. Here religion comes into action. The word religion comes from the *root're'*, meaning '*back*', and '*ligare*,' meaning '*to bind*.' Thus religion is the way, which binds people back with God. At first people enjoyed the blessings of nature as children do, without deeply analyzing the causes and actions. It was sufficient for them that the earth gave them cereals to feed and herbs to heal. They were contented that the trees bore them fruit and the streams quenched their thirst. They were happy, and every moment though unconsciously they offered a prayer of gratitude to the Supreme whom as yet they did not know. But later, in some religions, this turned quite complex when people started offering sacrifices and made rites and ceremonies an essential part of it to obtain special rewards from the Supreme. So today, when we look about, we find hundreds of philosophies and religions describing the path to God in their own special way. Still, the purpose of all religions, whether practiced since the beginning of human society or in the current perspective, is the same – to help followers know God. There may be a difference in rituals, prayers and other religious practices, but they all have grown on the same pathway of desire to meet the Supreme Creator.

In the history of religion, there is one practice, which has been known for its simplicity and also for its secret approach. This is Sufi Mysticism. The word *Sufi* is derived from the Arabic word '*suf*' which means '*wool*' and this refers to the coarse woolen robes that were worn by the followers of *Sufi* Mysticism. Although, in its larger sense, the word *Sufi* Mysticism is difficult to define, yet it can be said that it deals with some special experiences and speculations and these experiences are based on such material that is supposed to be beyond the reach of sense and reason.

The earliest account of the principles of *Sufi* Mysticism is found in the teachings of Sheikh Aby Saiyad [967 AD-?] and Abdul Majad Sanahi [?-1030 AD]. According to them, a true follower of *Sufi* Mysticism is the one who gets devoted to the Supreme in such a way that he forgets himself and as such agrees with the will of Supreme.

But the detailed account of *Sufi* Mysticism is found in the teachings of Saint Abdul Qadir Jilani [1077-1166 AD]. He was also known by the name of *Peeran-i-Peer,* which literally means the Saint of Saints. His main teachings are compiled in two popular books–*Al Fathal Rabbani* and *Futuh-al-Ghaib*. In them he has explained the vanity of external practices of worship. He laid emphasis on the purity of thought and action. He said that as such the true devotion in the Supreme develops. He also said that the war we fight against our egoistic hearts is the holiest. He propounded that a true devotee of God is the one who while leading a family life keeps himself free of all the vices of the world.

But later, in India, when people were guided through the teachings of Khwaja Moinuddin Chishti [1139-1236 AD], *Sufi* Mysticism became a popular means of attaining purity of soul. He selected the town of Ajmer as his permanent abode. He taught:

"A sin committed does not harm an individual so much as looking down upon one's own fellow human beings. Of all the worship that pleases Almighty, the most is the granting of relief to the humble and oppressed."

His shrine later became a place of pilgrimage largely with the support of Muslim rulers. The Moghul emperor, Akbar used to have annual pilgrimage there.

Then Sheikh Farid [1173-1265 AD], who was born near Multan in the present Pakistan, was greatly inspired by his mother's advice to seek God instead of the world, because the world had nothing worthwhile to offer and whatever little it did, could not be retained after death. He undertook rigorous self-discipline and physically punishing methods to gain Supreme-realization. Eventually he was advised to go to Qutub-ud-Din Bakhtiyar Kaki of Delhi, who finally revealed to him the Mystic path. In his work that was later constituted in the Adi Granth of Sikhs, Sheikh Farid revealed the secrets of Sufi Mysticism in a very easy fashion. He shaded the land of Punjab with the beauty of his thought and experience. He laid emphasis on the following basic principles for self-purification:

1. One should be polite and should consider others superior than him;

2. One should consider himself as a servant to God and as such should believe that God is watching over him; and

3. One should be obedient to his Spiritual Master because without his grace, self-restraint was not possible.

He said:

"Do not speak harshly to any one, as the Lord is in all; do not break anyone's heart as all are precious pearls."

What is that knowledge, virtue and thing

Which is dear to the spouse?

What dress should be put on to win over the Lord?

Humility is the knowledge, simplicity the virtue

And sweet-tongue the winning chant that are dear to Him.

If the dress of all these three is put on, the Lord is won over.

During his time, high rank people used to keep slaves. Sufi Mystics were totally against that. So each time any royal official, governor or rich merchant came to pay a visit, Sheikh Farid asked them to free their slaves. People knew that *Sufi* Mystics were made happy by freeing slaves so to gain their admiration; a new disciple used to free his slaves at once and even encouraged his fellowmen to do the same. It is also known that money was offered to him in hundreds of thousands but he used to spend every single penny for the welfare of the poor and needy.

His disciple and successor, Hazrat Nizamuddin Aulia [1236-1325 AD] also carried out this effort successfully. He used to say:

"God holds dear those, who love Him for the sake of Human beings; and also those who love human beings for the sake of Almighty God."

The well-known *Sufi* Saint of Punjab, Hazrat Miyan Meer [1550-1635 AD] also emphasized:

"The mind should be purified by abstaining from suspicion, plotting and thinking ill of others. The

heart should be purified by keeping it free from lust, jealousy, greed, selfishness, hatred and pride."

Prince Dara Shikoh [1615-1659 AD], who was the son of Moghul emperor Shahjahan, was also a follower of *Sufi* Mysticism. His early education was entrusted to tutors attached to the royal court. In his life, he came in contact with numerous Muslim and Hindu mystics. But the most noted among them was Hazrat Miyan Mir of Lahore who made the prince his disciple. In his book, *Risala-i-Haqnama*, he has written that Sufi Saints believed in some exclusive principles like:

1. Awakening of hidden spiritual powers through unconditional surrender and submission before Supreme;

2. Attainment of enlightenment through the initiation by a True Spiritual Master; and

3. That the Supreme Himself incarnates as a Spiritual Master to guide people on the pathway of eternal liberation of a soul.

In his collection of poems, *Iksir-i Azam*, he said:

"Whatever you behold except Him is the object of your fancy,

Things other than He have an existence like a mirage.

The existence of God is like a boundless ocean,

People are like forms and waves in its water."

He was a responsible and sincere Muslim prince, whose efforts were to find a common ground between Hindu and Muslim religious thoughts. He was quite popular among the *Rajput* Kings. Although, during his father's serious illness, there broke out a fight for succession among brothers, he was considered to be the rightful heir to the throne, but was defeated and arrested by his own brother, Aurangzeb. Later, he was prosecuted and sentenced to death.

Then, Bulleh Shah [1680-1758 AD], the Mystic poet from Punjab, was the most popular Sufi of his times. His poems are full of love and longing for God and his Spiritual Master. In his poetry, he has also denounced ritualistic religion and stressed on developing the feeling of oneness and brotherhood. He said:

"Remove duality and do away with all disputes;

The Hindus and Muslims are not other than Him.

Deem everyone virtuous, there are no thieves.

For, within every body He Himself resides."

So, in India, they were *Sufi* Mystics such as Khwaja Moinuddin Chishti, Sheikh Farid, Nizamuddin Auliya, Miyan Mir, Bulleh Shah, and many others, who devoted their lives in spreading the light of equality among all people, irrespective of their native, social or religious origin. They left for all men, a rich tradition of love and peace for all times. Thus it can be said that *Sufi* Mysticism in India has commonly been viewed as a secular attempt for eternal quest of the soul and for its direct experience of the ultimate Supreme. For centuries, Hindus have also accepted *Sufi* shrines as a symbol of communal harmony. A large number of them have been offering prayers in *Sufi* shrines. Even today, their teachings are a source of light in the dark and guidance for the seekers of truth. Indeed, through the unconditional surrender to the Will of God and through the feeling of brotherhood, this world hopes to enjoy eternal peace and harmony.

Bibliography:

- Al-Ghazzali, The Book of Knowledge, George Allen and Unwin Ltd, London [U. K.], 1970
- Anand, B. S. Baba Farid, *Sahitya Akademi*, New Delhi [India], 1975
- Burckhardt, Titus, An Introduction to Sufism. Aquarian Press, 1990
- Currie, P. M. The Shrine and Cult of Moinuddin Chishti of Ajmer, Oxford University Press, Delhi [India], 1989
- Nizami, K. A., The Life and Times of Shaikh Nizam-u'd-Din Auliya, Idarah-i Adabiyat-I, Delhi [India], 1991

- Rizvi, Saiyad Athar Abbas, A History of Sufism in India, 2 Volumes, Munshiram Manoharlal Publishers Pvt. Ltd., Delhi [India], 1978
- Schimmel, Annemarie, *Sufi* literature, Afghanistan Council of the Asia Society, New York [U. S. A.], 1975
- Shah, Idries, Tales of the Dervishes, Teaching-Stories of the Sufi Masters Over the Past Thousand Years, New York [U. S. A.], 1970
- Teg Bahadur, Guru, *Shabdarath Sri Guru Granth Sahib, Shromani Gurdwara Prabandhak* Committee, Amritsar, Punjab [India] 1999

****

GLOSSARY OF INDIAN TERMS

Abhyas	:	Practice
Ashram	:	Hermitage; abode of spiritual teacher; place for disciplined community; one of the four stages in the life of Vedic-Hindus
Banka	:	A toy of curved shape
Bhagvad-Gita, the	:	The song celestial, highly philosophic verses lying emphasis on the selfless view of life and action
Bhava	:	Existence; life; birth; origin; world; a title of Lord Shiva, one of the three supreme gods of Vedic-Hindus
Bhillini	:	A women of a tribal people of ancient India
Bhikshuka	:	A beggar; a holy man living by begging alms; a Buddhist Monk
Bhoga	:	Enjoyment; pleasure in food; sexual intercourse or enjoyment; gratification
Brahmin	:	One belonging to priestly class among the Vedic-Hindus
Buniyadi	:	Basic; fundamental
Chakshu	:	Eye

Chandala	:	A class engaged in butchery in the ancient period
Cheevar	:	Garment of an ascetic; upper garment of a Buddhist Monk
Chingulia	:	A kind of toy
Dharma	:	Behaviour; deeds; duty; feeling; religious Injunction
Dhanuhi	:	A bow-shaped toy
Dukkha/Dukha	:	Distress; grief; sorrow; suffering :
Gandha	:	Smell; fragrance; scent; perfume
Gariya	:	A cart-shaped toy
Ghrana	:	Smelling; fragrance
Himsa	:	Violence; violent treatment or conduct; outrage
Jatila	:	A matted [as hair]
Jivha	:	The tongue
Jnana	:	Knowledge
Kama	:	Desire; sexual-desire; passion: lust; object of desire; action; act; work; task; occupation
Karmana	:	In the deed; of action
Karunaparamita	:	Compassion of the highest order
Kaya	:	Body
Kheer	:	A dish of rice boiled in milk with sugar
Khasttriya	:	One belonging to the worrier class; one of the four Varnas of the Vedic-Hindu Society

Lattu	:	A kind of toy; knob; door-knob
Mahatma	:	A high-souled person; a title bestowed on Gandhi
Mana	:	Mind
Manasa	:	In the mind
Mara	:	Satan; device; tempter
Maryada Purushottama	:	Ethically restricted excellent person; an attribute to Lord Rama
Nagarvadhu	:	A city-bride
Nandi	:	Rejoicing; name of the bull of Shiva
Navadhabhakti	:	Knowledge of nine divisions [kinds] of devotion as propounded by Lord Rama to Bhillini-Shabari
Paramita	:	That reached to the far shore
Prana/Pran	:	Life; soul; spirit; vital air; breath
Raga	:	Passion
Ramarajya	:	Divine rule; the kingdom of God
Rasa	:	Heap; noise; din; pile; dance of cowherds
Roopa	:	Appearance; shape; form; beauty; aspect; features
Saddharma	:	The true dharma
Sadhana	:	To achieve-by work or devotion; to accomplish; study; learning
Samskara	:	Instinct; adorning; refining
Sanatana Dharma	:	The old rule

Sangha	:	Group; association; body; party; federation; union; a community of Buddhist Monks
Satya	:	Truth
Senapati	:	An army chief; general; high ranking commander; commander-in-chief
Shabda	:	Sound; word; noise; word of God
Shreshthiputra	:	Son of a prominent businessman or merchant
Shrota	:	A listener; hearer; audience
Shloka	:	Metrical verse of composition; couplet
Sparsha	:	A touch; feel; contact
Trishna	:	Desire
Tula	:	A pair of scales; weighting as a test of guilt or innocence; Libra; vessel for measuring grain
Vacha	:	In the word
Vaishya	:	One belonging to trading class; one of the four Varnas of the Vedic-Hindu Society
Vaishnava	:	A follower or devotee of Vishnu
Vedic	:	Pertaining to Vedas-the most sacred and ancient scriptures of the Vedic-Hindus, four in number
Vigraha	:	Separation; quarrel; strife
Vigyana	:	Science; acquired knowledge [of the world]
Yajna	:	Sacrificial act; offering; sacrifice

Yoga : Union; connection; combination; agreement; a theory or practice of abstract meditation undertaken to bring towards or into union with the supreme authority; bodily exercises; one of the prominent branches of the Vedic-Hindu Philosophy, established by Patanjali

****